Conversations
with Poppi about
GOD

Conversations with Poppi about GOD

An Eight-Year-Old and Her Theologian
Grandfather Trade Questions

Robert W. Jenson
and Solveig Lucia Gold

Brazos Press
Grand Rapids, Michigan

Published by Brazos Press
a division of Baker Publishing Group
P.O. Box 6287, Grand Rapids, MI 49516-6287
www.brazospress.com

Printed in the United States of America

Library of Congress Cataloging-in-Publication Data

Gold, Solveig Lucia.
    Conversations with Poppi about God : an eight-year-old and her theologian grandfather trade questions / Solveig Lucia Gold and Robert W. Jenson.
        p.   cm.
    Includes bibliographical references.
    ISBN 10: 1-58743-186-6 (cloth)
    ISBN 978-1-58743-186-9 (cloth)
    1. Theology, Doctrinal. 2. Gold, Solveig Lucia—Interviews. 3. Jenson, Robert W.—Interviews. I. Jenson, Robert W. II. Title.
BT77.G655 2006
230—dc22   2006007795

Contents

An Introductory Note by Solveig   7
An Introductory Note by Poppi   9

The Beginning   11

Why the Apple?   12

Boring Heaven?   15

God-Talk   16

Earth, Air, Fire, and Water—and
    Some Soteriology   19

Evil   21

God, Jesus, and Lucifer   24

Jesus, God's Other Children, and
    Some Epistemics   26

God's Teasing   27

Santa Claus   28

God's Motives   29

Communion Practices   31

A Weird Bishop   34

Baptism and the Spirit   35

Rearranging the Trinity   39

Providence   42

The Messiah   45

Time Machines   47

Contents

On Propositions Contrary to Fact and Disobeying Rules   49

The Crucifixion   51

The Image of God   55

On Christian Origins   56

Indulgences and What Followed   62

Church Divisions   68

On Christian Origins Again   71

Some Metaphysics   73

The Resurrection and Angels   74

Angels, the Spirit, and Our Minds   77

David and Solomon   81

The Land of Israel   85

Santa Claus and Other Saints   87

Calendars and Ritual   92

Trinitarian and Incarnational Matters   99

Man Ist Was Man Isst   107

Economics   109

Prayer, Works, and Hamsters   114

The Lord's Prayer   125

Further to the Lord's Prayer   127

The Nicene Creed   134

Time and Eternity   142

Back to the Creed   143

Lent   148

John the Baptist   152

Forty Days and Forty Nights   154

Anything More?   158

An Introductory Note
by Solveig

It all began on a dark, chilly night, sitting by the fireplace long after my bedtime at Mimi and Poppi's home in Princeton, New Jersey. I had a theological question to ask my grandfather (Poppi). It was autumn of 2003. I was eight years old at the time. I don't remember what the question was, seeing as it is now August 30, 2004, but I do remember that Poppi gave a lengthy reply that led me to ask him more theological questions.

The next morning, Mimi (my grandmother) suggested that Poppi and I have more conversations and record them to turn them into a book. By the way, the reason I asked Poppi the question to begin with is because he is the Reverend Canon Professor Dr. D. Robert W. Jenson, B.A., B.D., M.A., D.Theol., D.H.L., D.D. You might have noticed what a rather long title that is. Well, all I can say is that it goes with his lengthy replies.

As you can see, we went through with the plan. We went to Radio Shack and bought a cassette recorder. From then on, every weekend I was in Princeton, we would discuss theology. When we finished, Mimi listened to what had been recorded and typed it. She wrote down everything, including when I asked Poppi if the tape recorder was working properly. Speaking of which, there was a day when we had a wonderful conversation and then realized we hadn't recorded it. That was very frustrating.

To find out more, well, you'll have to read the book!

—Solveig Lucia Gold
August 30, 2004

An Introductory Note
by Poppi

The following records the wholly unscripted exchanges between an eight-year-old theologian and a seventy-three-year-old theologian.

The sessions went very much as you will read them. It fell to me, following transcription, to edit. I deleted chatter about the recorder. I have retained a selection of "Well, but . . ." "You know . . ." and the like for flavor, but eliminated many; in face-to-face conversation, such things, along with tone of voice and body language, serve communication, but on a page, they are just verbal filler. Where because of a speaker's incoherence (which happened to both of us once or twice) or failures of recording (Solveig kept spinning around in her chair and I kept leaning back) only a meaningless jumble could be recovered, I have removed it. And I have remedied some of my own worst lapses of diction—only, of course, for the reader's sake.

In the conversations, I did not think I should immediately correct every theological or historical error, Solveig's or mine, though some of mine are embarrassing. Nor have I done so now.

The subheadings scattered through the following text do not mark the beginnings of sessions. They mark the points at which somebody changed the subject, often—as readers should observe—because of an associational move from a subject under discussion.

Finally, why should anyone but our family read this book? From Plato on, it has been held that the first home of truth— theological or other—is lively conversation, and its second home the reading of such conversations' records. Moreover, that in this instance the two theologians are a churchgoing child and an academic professional seems to us to furnish this second home of truth in a specific way, a way perhaps useful to similar children, and those who must deal with them, and to similar scholars and those who must deal with them. Our advice: read as you would a Platonic dialogue, though in this one, the role of Socrates goes back and forth.

—Robert W. Jenson
October 2004

The Conversations

The Beginning

Poppi: What do you want to talk about?

Solveig: The beginning.

P: Okay. The beginning of what?

S: The world.

P: The whole world?

S: Why were we all created on different days?

P: You mean like in the story at the beginning of the Bible?

S: Right.

P: Well, if you'll look at the story, you'll see that it moves from less complicated things to more complicated. You start off with the big bang of light, then you get the sorting out of heavy and light stuff—water, earth, air—then you get plants, and then fish . . .

S: Why next fish?

P: You know something? The theory of evolution that Charles Darwin discovered has more or less the same order of things. Plants evolved first, then animals—and the first kind of animals were fish—and then birds . . . No, that's wrong—and then land animals. And then from our point of view, we're the most important, so we come last.

Why the Apple?

Solveig: So why did God try to tempt Eve to eat the apple?

Poppi: You know, in the story, it isn't God who tempts Eve to eat the apple . . .

S: The snake does. But why does God create a snake that would tempt Eve?

P: I don't know.

S: Sometimes I think it was better that he did that because otherwise we wouldn't exist.

P: Why wouldn't we?

S: Because there would be no reason to create other people.

P: That's interesting. Why would he need Eve to eat the apple to have a reason to create other people?

S: Well, if she hadn't eaten the apple, then she would live forever and ever, and so there wouldn't be any reason for us to exist.

P: You know, there are lots of people, including Christian theologians, who have said just that, Solveig—that for life to continue on the earth, which is only so big, you can't have people being born all the time without people dying at the other end.

S: Right.

P: If God wanted a succession of generations, there had to be death, and if there had not been a succession of generations, there would be no Solveig.

S: So what if the only reason he created us was he wanted companions? He didn't need an apple to create companions.

P: He could have been satisfied with just two people, you mean?

S: Right.

P: I suppose he could have been.

S: I think he wanted . . .

P: He wanted Solveig.

S: He wanted for there to be much more interesting things than just two people for the rest of his life.

P: That's right. He wanted Solveig and Poppi. Why he wanted *so* many we have to ask him.

S: How come with only two people—a male and a female—how come there could be so many children, and then they had more children, and then they all ended up in families?

P: That's how it would work, isn't it? Suppose Adam and Eve had four children—we don't know how many they had. The Bible mentions just two, but presumably they had more than that. They would have had to have girls, otherwise Cain and Abel wouldn't have found wives.

S: Right.

P: That makes four.

S: Wait! Who was the other son besides Abel?

P: Cain.

S: The book I was reading in August—there was a girl whose gardener was named Abel, and he had a brother named Cain. Cain almost killed Abel, but not quite. But in the Bible, he really did kill him.

P: If Adam and Eve had five children, and there were two living pairs from them, and if each of them had five . . .

S: Right.

P: You can see how it would work. According to some scientists, there was an "African Eve". . .

S: Scientists always make up weird things.

P: They say that sometime, probably in Africa, there came a point when there were not just pre-humans but humans like you and me. And at that point, there had to have been one woman who was the first ancestor of the whole human race.

S: Right.

14

Boring Heaven?

Solveig: So when we get to heaven and we're going to live forever, won't it get sort of tiresome? You'll be there forever and ever and ever and ever and ever . . .

Poppi: That isn't exactly what the Bible says.

S: All right . . .

P: It isn't as if the kingdom of God were just the same thing going on and on and on. When I was just about your age, I was sitting in a pew listening to the preacher, who happened to be my father. He was talking about heaven and hell, and I sat there thinking like you—if heaven just goes on and on and on, and hell goes on and on and on, there's not a whole lot of difference between them.

S: There's no pleasure at all.

P: But what the Bible really talks about finally is being taken into the life of God himself, and the life of God is just, as it were, one big excitement, a kind of explosion of excitement.

S: So it's like the excitement of getting something you have always wanted—that kind of excitement.

P: Or the excitement of giving something you've always wanted to give.

S: Or the excitement of sitting in your grandpa's lap.

P: You like that, do you? I'm happy. Now, you know, there is something to that. Just think about an absolutely perfect grandpa. Your present grandpa . . . (laughter)

S: You're pretty perfect.

P: Thank you very much, but only pretty perfect? An absolutely perfect grandpa . . .

S: Would be . . . An absolutely perfect grandpa would have to be . . .

P: God.

S: God is our *father*. So *he* would have to have a father, right?

P: Well . . . I don't suppose God is a father and a different grandfather . . . that could go on forever.

God-Talk

Solveig: So how do we have any idea of what God looks like? How do we have any image of God? How do we know what he is like?

Poppi: We know what he is like on account of Jesus.

S: Yes, but that was thousands and thousands . . .

P: Nevertheless, we do know about it.

S: But that was (pause) two thousand and three years ago.

P: Sure. But the story about him, what he did and what he was like, has kept on going. Moreover, according to the story, he didn't just die.

S: Right.

P: He died and rose again, so he's alive now . . .

S: Right. He's at the right hand of the Father.

P: So we do meet him from time to time.

S: Right. Right. When you say "right hand of the Father," he doesn't have a right hand, necessarily. It could be, I guess, his right *side*. But what if he doesn't have a right side?

P: There are two answers to that. One is that since Jesus is supposed to be God the Father all over again, there must be some sense in which God does have hands, because Jesus does.

S: But people say . . . How does it go? There was a song we sang to the first-graders in school this year. It says, "May he hold you forever in the palm of his hand." And our music teacher said he only needs one big hand to hold all of us in. He doesn't need two hands.

P: Okay.

S: He doesn't need two hands to lift a pizza up in the air. He can do that with one hand.

P: Or with no hands at all.

S: Right.

P: I said there were two answers . . .

S: Right.

P: One is that there must be some sense in which God does have hands because of Jesus. But the other is that—not *all*, by any means, but a good bit of—the language we use about God is what we call metaphor.

S: What does that mean?

P: It means that you use words to say something that the words you use really can't say.

S: Okay.

P: Like when Blanche[1] calls you Miss Muffet.

S: Yes.

P: You really aren't the Miss Muffet of the story.

S: No, I'm not.

P: And you are not sitting on a tuffet or eating curds and whey.

S: No.

P: But she wants to say something to you, a loving thing and a thing . . .

S: She wants to say how absurd I am!

P: That can't really get said except with this phrase, that you are Miss Muffet, even though you are not Miss Muffet. That's called a metaphor.

S: Right. So . . .

P: So if we say God is the rock of ages, he is not a piece of granite sitting in the river.

S: So you could step on him.

P: There *is* something about God that is rock-like.

S: Strong.

P: Strong, heavy . . .

1. Mimi, Solveig's grandmother and Poppi's wife.

Earth, Air, Fire, and Water— and Some Soteriology

Solveig: What if part of God is air? You can lift up air easily.

Poppi: God doesn't have any parts.

S: What I mean is, some of his body is air, some of it liquid, some of it solid . . .

P: Do you know what you just did?

S: What?

P: You reinvented the theology of some of the first Greek philosophers. (laughter) The Greek philosophers, at the very beginning of philosophy and theology, wondered what was the stuff of things. And what you just said is one way they thought about it.

S: Stuff?

P: What's real? That was their question. Some said air, some said earth, some said fire, and some said water. And finally they said probably all four. Both God and we are made up of air, fire, and water and earth.

S: Are we?

P: I don't think that's true, but . . .

S: But maybe gas is for us to breathe; then hell has fire and heaven has something else.

P: If I were going to do that, I'd do it the other way around.

S: Why?

P: I'd make heaven be fire so that it doesn't get dull. (laughter) And I'd make hell out of dull old earth.

S: But you wouldn't want lots of people in it. In the olden days, they used to say that hell was a pit of fire and that you have to jump into it.

P: But, you know, what they were thinking about was how if fire burns you, it hurts.

S: Right.

P: But what if you had a fire that didn't hurt?

S: A fire that didn't hurt would be just plain air filled with water that you could fly through.

P: It would be light, excitement. That would be a good metaphor for heaven.

S: Right. But then hell would have to be solid.

P: Clunky and dull.

S: Like a jail. Jails are horrid. They are solid; they have bars. Say you die. Your body is still here, and then your soul goes to heaven or hell. How can God pick who goes to heaven or hell?

P: By looking at Jesus, who loves *you*, Solveig.

S: Can you show me?

P: One way of saying what happened with Jesus is that Jesus so attached himself to you that if God the Father wants his Son, Jesus, he is stuck with you too. Which is how he picks you.

Evil

Solveig: Can you tell me the story of the devil and how he became so terrible?

Poppi: I can't tell you a story that I know to be true. The one that people tell is not in the Bible, you understand.

S: Right.

P: Well, besides earth and air, God wanted living things— plants, animals, people, and so on. Now, there is one way that there is a difference between your life and your body; if you die, your body is still there, but your life is gone. So the story is—I don't know if this is true or not, but it is the story that people have told—the story is that God wanted living things that were *only* life. Those are the angels.

S: And the devil was an angel, right?

P: The devil was the chief of the angels.

S: He was God's favorite angel.

P: He was called Lucifer, "the Bearer of Light."

S: And then Lucifer betrayed God.

P: Yes. And do you know the story about why he did it?

S: Why?

P: Because God made the angels before he made people. That's out of order, but that's how it is in the story.

S: But angels are more complicated than people.

P: That's why I say it's sort of out of order. Anyway, the way the story is told, God made the angels first. Then he told the angels he was going to make people. And they said, "What do you want them for? You have us." And God told the angels not only that he was going to make people but that he was to become himself one of those creatures. He would be a person as a human, Jesus, and not as an angel. Which made the angels very jealous: "If you are going to become a creature one day, you have to become one of us." And that was Lucifer's jealousy.

S: And so he was banished from heaven, right?

P: Right.

S: But he didn't want to be banished.

P: In the story, Lucifer didn't want anything more to do with such a stupid God as one who would make people and be one of them.

S: Well, it does seem sort of dumb sometimes . . . like creating storms, like creating brains that think of terrible things . . .

P: But brains are a very good idea, don't you think?

S: That would think of terrible things, brains that thought of death and war and all those . . .

P: Theologians talk about the problem of evil, meaning, Why does God let there be evil things?

S: Right. But then again, some of the evil things are for good causes.

P: That's true too.

S: So some wars are to get rid of terrible things.

P: But then why were there the terrible things in the first place to be gotten rid of?

S: And he created the brains that can do terrrible things, that created the bombs. Why?

P: Well, two answers. One is that we don't know. Lots of people refuse to believe in God at all on account of the existence of evil. One of the great novels—maybe the greatest of all—*The Brothers Karamazov* by Dostoyevsky, has a character—he's really the most interesting character in the novel—named Ivan. Ivan has a very saintly brother, and one day Ivan tells his brother the reason he is an atheist . . .

S: What's an atheist?

P: Someone who doesn't believe in God. The reason is that Ivan just doesn't want anything to do with a God who would let even one little girl be tortured. Now, that isn't stupid.

S: It isn't stupid. But in many ways it's okay to believe in something that could be terrible . . . Like you could believe in ghosts and witches in the world, and they are terrible. You could believe that kind of thing.

P: You don't though? Do you?

S: Well . . . no. My question is . . . We're getting off the subject of God, but if there are no witches and ghosts, how do they even get into people's minds? How do they believe in it and think, for instance, that someone is a witch?

P: People have a desperate need to explain things; it's part of what God created in us. Gretel[2] doesn't need to explain things.

S: No, she doesn't.

2. The family dog, an amiable and elderly Norwich terrier.

P: But we do.

S: Otherwise our brains will burst.

P: And there are lots of things that happen for which people have found the existence of witches the easiest explanation. When somebody gets sick, *we* say . . .

S: We've got a bug.

P: But how about before we knew about bugs?

S: But bugs were created very early.

P: Bugs were only *discovered* a few years ago, comparatively.

S: That's not exactly true, beause there were bugs . . .

P: But not the kind that make you sick, viruses and bacteria. So think of this scene: In a village, all of a sudden all the kids in one house get sick. The next-door neighbor is known to hate those kids because they make a lot of noise, and to have wished them dead. It's an explanation to say . . .

S: She's a witch.

P: And that somehow she has the power to make things like that happen. You see?

S: All right . . . Let's get back on the subject of theology.

God, Jesus, and Lucifer

Solveig: There's a lot of relation between God and Jesus. For instance, they were both betrayed by someone they trusted and whom they knew very well.

Poppi: God was betrayed by Lucifer in the one case. So . . .

S: It's like you said before. Jesus is the second God; he has a lot of the same things happen to him as what happened to . . .

P: The Father.

S: Right.

P: And that's how the Gospels tell the story too. I don't know if you have ever heard or paid attention to this passage in the Bible. You know, sometimes in church you're not paying attention . . .

S: I'm reading.

P: It says the devil entered into Judas and he betrayed Jesus. So it was, in fact, according to that part of the story, the same person who betrayed God both times. In fact, you might want to take it the other way around. What happened in this world that we can know about is that Judas betrayed Jesus. It's from this that we say that something like that must have happened at the beginning of things.

S: All right. But how could Lucifer have already been the chief of all the angels if it was only about two days . . .

P: You have to remember, this whole story about Lucifer is not in the Bible.

S: Right.

P: It's just a good story.

S: It's a prophecy. Right?

Jesus, God's Other Children, and Some Epistemics

Solveig: So if Jesus were God's Son . . .

Poppi: He *is* God's Son.

S: *Is* God's Son. But we're all God's sons and daughters, so he could have been—I guess—closer. It's sort of like if Joseph was his real father, he has the same relation with God as we do.

P: But that's backwards. We are God's sons and daughters because . . .

S: Of Jesus.

P: Because we are adopted to be his brothers and sisters. There is a metaphor here again. It's like in a family. Let me tell a story. There is a family, and they have one child—this is like your family or mine.

S: Right.

P: Only in this family, the child is a very unselfish child . . .

S: Doesn't sound like me. (laughter)

P: In this family, the child is a very unselfish child, and the child says to the parents, "I'm lonely. I would like to have sisters and brothers to share things with." But the parents say, "We're sorry, but we can't have any more children."

S: I'd like to have a sister or brother—maybe.

P: The child says, "A sister or brother would be nice." So on account of their natural child, they adopt other children, who really are sons and daughters also but are sons and daughters on account of the first son or daughter. That is something like the way it is with Jesus and God and with us.

S: Okay. So . . . this is sort of a funny question, but . . . This doesn't have much to do with anything in theology, it's just a question. Why do you think that *God* is the same as *dog* spelled backwards?

P: By sheer accident.

S: Do you think they knew that when they thought of *dog*?

P: Nope. That is just an accident in English.

S: Sure. Because in all the other languages . . .

P: In Latin, god is *deus* and dog is *canis*. No relationship.

S: So what do you think makes us so eager to ask all these questions?

P: Well, getting back to creation . . . As you said at the beginning, God made people to have companions. That means there had to be people who would ask questions, and ask questions about God. Look, you're Isabel's friend. If you didn't have any interest in finding out about Isabel . . .

S: Then we wouldn't be friends.

God's Teasing

Solveig: Do you think—this is sort of dumb, but anyway—that God sometimes teases us? He sits wherever heaven is and laughs at us when we do funny things? He teases us for doing foolish things?

Poppi: Yes. If God didn't have an immense sense of humor, he wouldn't put up with us at all.

S: (laughter)

P: And I think he also teases us—that is, provokes us from time to time.

S: Right. If we trip over a rug, he just sort of . . .

P: Laughs.

Santa Claus

Solveig: When people thought of Santa Claus—the idea of Santa Claus is very much like God . . .

Poppi: No. It's not.

S: Sort of. He's just very jolly and very . . .

P: Well, you see, there are two things about Santa Claus. *Sinter Klas* is Dutch for St. Nicholas. And there really was a St. Nicholas. He was a bishop who became famous for giving people things.

S: Right. But all the same . . .

P: He *is* a *little* bit like God . . .

S: Very much like God.

God's Motives

Solveig: If God is the king of the universe, how come we have kings and chiefs and presidents?

Poppi: The same way he wanted to have Solveigs and Poppis. You got it right the first time. He wants companions. We like to have companions who are different from us but also like us. Isabel is very much like you . . .

S: True. We were measuring each other the other day, and we were almost as tall as each other and our feet are the exact same size.

P: It's not just sizes, it's what you do, what you like. Now, supposing that there is a certain way in which God is everything. That's not to say that he is spread out like a big pudding, but that whatever there can be is already in God. So if there are kings, that is because God is king, and there are Solveigs because there is something sweet and charming in God. So to have companionship . . .

S: Right. And in some ways God is very selfish because he wanted the companionship. He didn't care if anyone else had companions. *He* wanted a companion.

P: Well, now, that's something theologians have debated for a long time. Does God create for his own sake or for our sake? Is he selfish or unselfish?

S: Both selfish and unselfish.

P: Precisely. By far the best answer was made by a man named Jonathan Edwards. In that God makes us for his own sake and loves us for his own sake, just so we are loveable, and so he loves us for our sake also. So both answers are right. Is God selfish? Yes. And perfectly unselfish? Yes.

S: Wait! Unselfish and selfish . . .

P: With God, they are the same.

S: Okay.

P: You can see how that would work. If you're perfectly selfish, you're unselfish and . . .

S: I guess . . . But does that mean that when people are selfish, he doesn't really mind because he . . .

P: Except the problem is we're never *perfectly* selfish. We're just trivially, meanly . . .

S: Selfish. When people take communion, it's the body and the blood of Jesus. Wasn't Jesus being, in a way, selfish by saying, "This is my body and blood, and do this for remembrance of me . . . I'm so great you must remember me"?

P: Yes. But remember also what is said: "This is the body of Christ, broken for *you*."

S: Right.

P: And, "This is the blood of Christ shed for *you*" and for everybody. So again, it's just the same thing we had with God.

S: Selfish and unselfish.

Communion Practices

Poppi: Now let me ask a question. You like to go to communion, don't you?

Solveig: My favorite part of going to church.

P: Why?

S: Well, I like getting up there, and sometimes I'm very thirsty during the service . . .

P: The wine you get with communion shouldn't quench much of your thirst.

S: I actually like going to communion because I get to stretch and walk around a little.

P: These are not very important reasons for going to communion.

S: I know, but that's why it's my favorite part of going to church. Actually, it's not my favorite part.

P: What's your favorite part? Sitting in the pew, reading a book and not paying any attention?

S: Yes. (laughter)

P: So what do you want to know about communion?

S: Well . . . what about how everybody sips from the same glass even though many people have germs and things? It's sort of odd. You pretty much think you're not going to get sick, but you never exactly know.

P: Do you want me to talk about that?

S: Yes.

P: All right, several points. First, there are all kinds of situations in which people drink from the same thing, as when a football team wins a championship. They just take the top off a bottle of Champagne and pass it around, right?

S: Yes.

P: Drinking out of the same vessel is a way of being one family together.

S: I know. But I think it's a good thing, anyway. Let's change the subject; I have nothing more to say about that.

P: Well, I do.

S: Okay.

P: First off, it's not odd, because it happens all the time wherever you have a group of people who make one thing together. Second, catching each other's germs is part of being one family together.

S: True.

P: When you get a cold, so does your mother, right?

S: Yes, or the other way around.

P: And third, the chances are very remote. There actually have been studies to see if people in congregations catch things from each other more than other people do.

S: One day at church, I was feeling quite normal in the morning, and then that Sunday after having communion, I vomited.

P: But if you had gotten it from the communion cup, it would have been a day and a half or so later.

S: That's why I wanted to know about germs and everything, because it was sort of odd it happened on the same day.

P: Communion cups are usually made out of silver plate and gold, and there's something about the reaction between wine and the metal that kills germs. It doesn't mean you couldn't catch something, but it's not very likely.

S: No. The other thing is I think the communion wine they serve is always a little too sweet.

P: I do too.

S: But wine isn't supposed to be sweet.

P: No. I agree—the wine should be the very best.

S: Yeah. It should be sour. And it should be something that is not just an everyday taste. The blood of Jesus should be a lot more exciting.

P: Like really good wine.

S: Yes.

P: Exactly.

S: I like really good wine!

P: Ahh . . . Yes.

S: I think we should cut this off, because it's not very important now.

P: I think it's very important. I'll tell you something else that I think is important. At some churches, the communion bread—usually, anyway—is real bread. Pita bread or something like that. I think that's better than little wafers.

S: Certainly. I don't like those little thingies you get.

P: They are not really like bread; they just dissolve on the tongue.

S: But some people like to dip; that's why they have them. Once, at the cathedral, they had that for Easter, and it wasn't very appetizing. But it is not supposed to be appetizing either.

P: *I* think it should be appetizing. Why not?

S: Well . . . It should be appetizing because it's supposed to be for people to like—not to absolutely despise communion. They want people to eat and drink. You don't want people to stay away from communion.

P: It's sort of like baptism when they just dribble a couple of drops on the baby.

S: Yes.

P: That's not really washing the baby, is it?

S: No.

A Weird Bishop

Solveig: I guess it was during the summer we had confirmation, and the guy who did it was this weird bishop guy; he wasn't really a bishop, or if he was, he was really stupid. And he had this really weird way of confirming people that Mommy and Daddy and I didn't like at all. He said something different for everyone.

Poppi: I think Blanche and I were there too.

S: You were?

P: Yes.

S: Well, he said different things for everybody . . .

P: And since he didn't know all these people, he didn't really have different things to say; he just made things up.

S: It was as if he had never confirmed anyone before.

P: Why do you suppose he did that? I thought it was stupid too, but why did he do it?

S: Maybe because he thinks that in God's eyes we're all so wonderful that he just wanted to show our splendor and so said something different for each. But if he really wanted to show our splendor . . . Because we are all one family, you would think he would have done it more the same for everybody.

Baptism and the Spirit

Solveig: Bring up something.

Poppi: Let's talk about communion some more.

S: Okay. But why don't we talk about baptism? That's a lot more interesting as a conversation.

P: You think so? Why?

S: Well, communion to me is just one basic fact; baptism has more of a story to it.

P: What story?

S: Like the story of why baptism became baptism.

P: And what's that story?

S: I want you to tell it to me.

P: The idea of washing someone to make them clean is a sort of obvious one, isn't it?

S: Yes . . . Clean of what?

P: That is the point.

S: Clean of evil.

P: Clean of evil or whatever you want. Strictly speaking, all that water does is to take dirt off. But that makes it an obvious symbol of getting rid of anything that feels dirty. When we know we have been up to things we shouldn't have been, we feel a bit dirty.

S: Yes.

P: So many religions have used water and washing as a symbol for starting over again, getting rid of all the old dirt and starting clean.

S: That's what the Jews celebrate on Yom Kippur.

P: Now, in Jesus's time, in Israel there were groups of Jews who had developed different ways of ritual washing. One of them was the group around a man named John the Baptist. Remember him?

S: Yes—which is why it's called baptism.

P: *Baptize* is just Greek for "wash," so to baptize someone is to wash them. John the Baptist was out in the wilderness calling on people to repent—that is to say, calling on people to start over, to get rid of their old dirt, to start afresh. As a way of doing that, he called them to come out to be washed in the River Jordan. And Jesus too went to be baptized.

S: Yes. Of course, there was nothing for him to wash away, exactly.

P: And everyone has always been puzzled why he did it.

S: Maybe he wanted to encourage people? And . . . we don't know, but maybe he wanted to give John the Baptist a blessing?

P: Can you think of anything else?

S: I'm sure I could if you give me about two minutes.

P: Okay, you've got your two minutes. (long pause)

S: Maybe he had never met John the Baptist.

P: He could have met John without being baptized.

S: Maybe he thought that he wanted to start over even if he had done it wonderfully. He could have just wanted to start over and do things differently than he had done before, even if he had done it wonderfully.

P: That's very good, I think. Do you remember what happened when Jesus was baptized?

S: What?

P: Well, he had just been washed, and he is standing there in the river with the water up to his knees. And then he had a vision of the heavens opening, and he heard God the Father saying, "This is my beloved Son. Listen to him." And he saw a dove as a symbol of the Holy Spirit joining him and God the Father. Right after that is when he began to preach and teach and heal people. So the baptism really was a way of ending one way of living—even if it was a wonderful way—and taking up a new beginning.

S: Okay. One other question: What is the Holy Spirit? Because you say Father, Son, and Holy Spirit, but how can the Holy Spirit really be anything?

P: We say that someone is very spirited . . .

S: It means they have a lot of happiness. They are not so glum about everything or dull—like in the *Phantom Toll Booth*.

P: Right. So anybody who is lively . . .

S: Has spirit.

P: So don't you suppose that God is livelier than anybody?

S: I'm sure he sees when you stumble on the street and says, "There goes that old professor again."

P: God's Spirit, the Holy Spirit, is God's liveliness. When we say someone is lively, we don't mean they jump up and down all by themselves, but that they get other people involved. Right?

S: Right. "I'm begging you, come over here. It's wonderful. Celebrate!"

P: So you talk about a sports team having spirit.

S: Right. And that's when they drink the one big bottle together.

P: Right! If a sports team didn't have a common spirit, they wouldn't have any fun playing together, and they wouldn't play very well, either. The quarterback in the football game has to know where the people he wants to catch the ball are going to be; there has to be a kind of wordless communication between them, a common liveliness, a common goal.

S: So we need a common goal to be happy.

P: Exactly. So the Spirit is God's liveliness. Now, there is another point, and this is the complicated one. If *I* am lively, my liveliness is not itself a person.

S: No. Your *liveliness* is the spirit.

P: But in God's case, his liveliness is God all over again.

S: Right. And . . .

P: That makes three. There is Jesus and his Father and . . .

S: Their Liveliness. Father, Son, and Spirit.

P: Does that help you any?

S: Yes. That helps.

Rearranging the Trinity

Solveig: When you say Father, Son, and Holy Spirit, do you think Spirit should come between them?

Poppi: What?

S: Father, Holy Spirit, Son. Jesus is more important than the Holy Spirit, but since the Spirit is something the Father and the Son share, shouldn't it be between them? The Holy Spirit is like their love. So why does it go after? Shouldn't it be between them?

P: I think so too.

S: Of course, Father, Holy Spirit, and Son is harder to say, but if you had been brought up to say Father, Holy Spirit, and Son, it would be easier to say than Father, Son, and Holy Spirit. That makes some sense.

P: You can very well say Father, Spirit, and Son. Or for that matter you could say Spirit, Son, and Father.

S: Yeah. But I think it should be between them—like a heart. When you see drawings of two people loving each other, you see the heart between them. That's what the Holy Spirit is—the heart, the love.

P: Good. We can agree on that.

S: Yes. I hope we can.

P: Why do you think we got started saying it the other way?

S: That's a good question. For crossing yourself, it doesn't work as well as Father, Son, and Holy Spirit.

P: I don't think it would make a difference there.

S: I guess it wouldn't make a difference. But what if they thought the Holy Spirit is something that everybody has, so they don't want to put it between God and Jesus? Because all of us share in the Spirit?

P: I think that is *part* of the reason. In the Apostles' Creed, the first article is the Father, and the second article is the Son, and the third article is the Spirit. The third article is "I believe in God, the Holy Spirit"; the first article is "I believe in God the Father Almighty"; the second one is "in Jesus Christ his only Son."

S: The Apostles' Creed was built out of Father, Son, and Holy Spirit. But maybe, because Father and Son are more important than the Holy Spirit . . . But that doesn't actually work, because Jesus wouldn't be kind and wonderful if it weren't for the Holy Spirit. It has nothing to do with importance, because actually the Holy Spirit is more important than either God or Jesus.

P: From one point of view . . .

S: Well, maybe not more important than God, because there would be no Holy Spirit if there were no God or Jesus.

P: But you interrupted me.

S: Right . . . But I also thought up something. God and his Holy Spirit together brought Jesus to Mary. If God hadn't had the Holy Spirit, Jesus wouldn't be there. And that's probably why they put Jesus between God and the Holy Spirit, because Jesus is born from God and the Holy Spirit—and of course Mary, but Mary doesn't appear there, unfortunately. Keep going.

P: Me?

S: Yes.

P: My turn. Well . . . look . . . God, the Father is what everything starts off with, right?

S: Yes.

P: So we name him first. And then we say that the Spirit is God's liveliness. When we say someone is lively, we mean they are looking forward, that there are things that they are interested in. Being lively is being directed to the future. So God as the Spirit is God's own future that he is looking forward to.

S: That's why it's after? So why is he looking forward? Is it because he gets to see all these weird people walking around?

P: Like you and me, you mean.

S: You especially.

P: I don't think I'm any weirder than you are, actually. I'm sitting here quite properly, and you are sitting there curled up like a tree frog or something. (laughter)

S: Yeah, but you stumble on the street. I don't think it is much liveliness when God looks forward to teasing people. I don't think he really has that much spirit to look *forward* to anything.

P: I think you are thinking about God as too much like a know-it-all.

S: He *is* a know-it-all.

P: Well, there is something wrong with that . . .

S: Know-it-all doesn't necessarily mean bad.

Providence

Solveig: I'm sure he knew everything that we think of. I'm sure he knew way back in the twelve-hundreds there would be electricity. I'm sure he knew about calculus before there was even math.

Poppi: What would you say if I suggested this? That undoubtedly God knew in twelve hundred that there is electricity and that someday people would discover it.

S: Right. But he didn't know when.

P: I'm sure he knew that too. But that people *would* discover it is something he left up to the people to do.

S: He was smart to do that. He was quite smart to do that.

P: How so?

S: Well . . . he knew that people don't want to be just pushed around. He knew that if he left it up to people, they could figure it out in their own strange way. If he had everything his way, he would never be interested.

P: That's exactly right. And it's not just people. All the planets, galaxies, stars, animals, black holes, and all the things you learn about in school—all that is exciting. God's excited by it. He wouldn't have done it if he were not interested in it.

S: Do you think God shares your excitement? When you read such a fabulous part of a book or when you get something you have wanted for a while or when you see someone get something, do you think he shares in your excitement?

P: Yes. I think he is more excited than I am.

S: Why?

P: Because he really knows what's going on, and I . . .

S: And he also sees your excitement, which makes him happy. Well, that's more like Jesus. Jesus is more of a kind person than God.

P: Oh, come now!

S: Yes.

P: Why did you say that?

S: Because of all the things God has created. But I seriously don't think that he created the people who have done all those bad things—which is going back to what we talked about before. He didn't create all things horrible; he just created confusion, and not by something he did. It was because people believed in something that people thought terrible things.

P: It's very hard for us to know why all the things there are were created.

S: Yeah. God created all of us for his own excitement, but I think that there was also some deep reason, a reason that we'll never know. Not because he wanted enjoyment. I think he wanted something that he couldn't have but that we will never know about—forever, practically. What do you think?

P: I think we do know what it is. I think it is Jesus.

S: Maybe we know what it is, but we don't know that we know what it is, if you know what I mean. Like, for instance, maybe for your birthday your mom said, "Well, honey, wouldn't you like the game Life?" So you heard of what you like; you heard what you were going to get for your birthday, but you don't exactly know you're going to get it.

P: That's just right. What we have heard we're going to get for our whole lives is Jesus.

S: So you think that's the reason he created us—for Jesus?

P: Yes.

The Messiah

Solveig: Okay. Now I want to talk about something else. I want to talk about David.

Poppi: David? David the king of Israel? That is a switch.

S: Yes, It is quite a big switch, but just talking about how Jesus was created made me think about that person who went up to David and said he was the great, great, great, great, great grandfather of the wonderful person who was coming, God's Son.

P: I don't know that anybody ever did that to David.

S: Yes.

P: Samuel came to David and said that he was to be the king of Israel. And once David was king of Israel, prophets told David that there would always be a descendant of his on the throne of Israel.

S: Right. But one time when Daddy was telling me the story, he said that before David was king, someone said that his descendant would be God's Son.

P: I suppose you could read the story that way. So go on.

S: Now here's my question: What if Jesus was before we know he was, exactly? What if that was his second time on earth? What if he had been born ages ago? And what if he's going to do that again when it is time to end the world? Which I don't really think God would do, because it would take all the fun out of it for the dead people.

P: I think your last point is right. Christians and Jews don't have this idea of people being born over and over again, because we think that each person's life is vital and important just as it is; you don't have to do it over again later on for it to be important. There's a great difference in religions at this point. For example, the Buddhists think that a Buddha shows up on the earth repeatedly.

S: Here is what I think is a little odd. If God created the earth for Jesus, why would he have made Jesus millions of years after he created the earth?

P: To give time for some others to be around as well.

S: And if he decides he likes the ones who showed up—or not?

P: Suppose Jesus had shown up and he was the only one here.

S: It wouldn't be much fun for Jesus or God.

P: That's right, it wouldn't have meant anything.

S: No. That's why I'm saying . . . What if he had been born the year after creation? Or what if he had been born that

46

very year? If he was Adam and Eve's son? If Adam and Eve's story is not a myth?

P: Well, it is a sort of myth, but we can talk about that later. Look, there are all kinds of questions like that. If Jesus had come right away, then people would ask, Why didn't God wait a while?

S: They wouldn't have known anything.

P: Whenever something happens, that's when it happens. Why did God choose the Jews? Why not the Egyptians? Because he chose the Jews. Why Mary instead of Sarah? Because he chose Mary. The way a thing happens is the way it happens, and that's all you can say.

S: Right.

Time Machines

Solveig: Now here's my question. How do you think time machines came in? Do you think people have had brilliant ideas to make time machines but have just never been able to do it? Or . . .

Poppi: That's not a theological question; we're supposed to be discussing theology.

S: Well . . . I know we are. I'm just . . .

P: There aren't any time machines, for one thing.

S: Right. People like hearing about different things that never happen. How do we know? Because that's what we were saying. God knows everything, but we don't. And so how will we know if there is not going to be a time machine? Or we might say, "Oh, I don't think elephants are going to fly."

P: Elephants *are* never going to fly. If elephants grew wings and flew, they wouldn't be elephants.

S: They would be called elewings!

P: Or whatever. Now, there aren't any time machines . . .

S: People like to hear stories.

P: There *might* be time machines . . .

S: Right. We don't know what is going to happen; only God knows what is going to happen.

P: There was a piece in the newspaper this morning about the possibility of time travel.

S: Are you serious? What did they talk about?

P: Well, according to the general theory of relativity, it would be possible for space and time to be so warped by matter that there would be something like tunnels in space and time, so you could go in at one end of one of those tunnels and come out at the other end a thousand years in the future or in the past.

S: But could you go, like, two years ago?

P: I don't know.

S: That would be interesting. I think that all the peace protestors would like that.

P: I think it would be a disaster.

S: Because everybody would want to change everything.

P: There's a paradox: What happens if you go into the past and shoot your own grandmother?

S: You wouldn't even know it was your grandmother.

P: Then you would never have been born, and if you had never been born, you wouldn't have gone into the past and shot your own grandmother.

S: Yes, and then you can't do it again.

P: That's called a paradox. So theoretically, there might be time travel, but there are reasons that there won't be.

On Propositions Contrary to Fact and Disobeying Rules

Solveig: I don't want there to be time machines anyway.

Poppi: Neither do I.

S: I find it a lot more interesting to talk about time machines than to have them in reality. If you talked about unicorns, you would have no interest in them if it was an everyday thing.

P: What you are saying is that some things are interesting because they can't happen.

S: Right. If everything can happen, then what's the point of having stories? What's the point of even living? What's the point of new people being born all the time? If everything could happen, there would only be two people on earth, if you know what I mean.

P: I'm not sure I know what you mean, but I'm sort of guessing at it.

S: If anything could happen, there would be no fun, and you wouldn't know . . .

P: The moral that follows from this is that rules about what is not to be done are necessary. If there were no rules about what we shouldn't do, nothing would be much fun.

S: This makes me think of a book, about a girl named Ruby Holler. I have not read the book, but I have the tape.

P: I notice you are shying away from my moral.

S: No. I'm just saying that where she grew up, everything had to have rules, and not for a very good reason. And they get sick and tired of the rules, and that made them break the rules. So in some ways, rules are awful. It depends on *what* rules; rules can make you not want to do *anything*.

P: But on the other hand, even if you break the rules, they make life more interesting by giving you something to break. It wouldn't be any fun to slide down the banister if you had never been told not to do it.

S: I know that. But here's the thing: in some cases, it's not fun to have rules. If you have a rule saying things like you should never read a book, that's a stupid rule isn't it?

P: It depends on what book you have in mind.

S: Matilda.

P: You are thinking of a character in a book named Matilda?

S: Right.

P: So why would anyone make a rule not to read?

S: In the book, the parents love TV.

P: This is a very modern book.

S: Yes. It's by Roald Dahl, and they only watch TV, and they won't even let the children eat a carrot. They won't even let her go to the library and read a book—even if it was bad TV, they wouldn't let her read a book.

P: This is sort of a reversal of what parents usually do. Mostly they want their children to read a book and not watch TV. Right?

S: Yes. My point has to do with having rules. It's not because of the rule; Matilda just doesn't want to watch TV.

P: You know something, Solveig, I think we have run this conversation out. Have you got another subject you want to talk about, or shall we just call it a day?

S: Well, I think we should continue. Let's keep talking.

The Crucifixion

Poppi: What do you want to talk about?

Solveig: I want to talk about the crucifixion.

P: Do you want me to just start talking about the crucifixion, or . . .

S: Yes. And then I'll interrupt and ask questions.

P: Well, Jesus was crucified because, as people said, he made himself out to be the Son of God.

S: Well, yes, he was crucified because of that. I'm sure if he had his choice, he would have refused to be crucified, but . . .

P: No. That's not true.

S: Well, yes, he did it for us. But then, if he had his choice, he would have done something for us that would make him not die.

P: Well, that's probably not right either. Remember the night before he was crucified? He was in the garden praying. He had just had his last supper with the disciples, and he went off by himself.

S: How do you know that is what he did?

P: It's in the Gospels.

S: Yes, but Jesus didn't write the Gospels.

P: No, but his disciples did.

S: Right—Matthew, Mark, Luke, and John. Wait . . . No, just go on.

P: And Jesus prayed, "Father if it be possible, let this cup pass from me," but then, "Not what I want, but what you want." You see, the thing about Jesus was that there really was nothing to his life but obedience to his Father, as he called God.

S: I think we talked about this a while ago, how some people might think Jesus was a little arrogant when you hear him say, "Take this and do this in remembrance of *me*."

P: So what's the matter with that?

S: Well, when he says to God, "What *you* want," if you didn't know any better, you would say he's just trying to show off to God: "Oh, Father . . ." That's what you would probably think if you didn't know any better.

P: But you know better.

S: Right.

P: The thing is, Jesus always said that having to die for us belongs to what he had been sent for. That was clear to him from the beginning. Now, why do you suppose that is so?

S: God wanted Jesus to show everybody else about him. Even if he knew that Moses would tell everyone about him, he wanted Jesus to be his messenger.

P: So why would that have to involve dying?

S: For there really to be a communication between you and God, you have to be able to meet him, not just sit around all day praying to him. Or . . . in praying, you do have a communication with him, but you don't have any actual moments of speaking to him; most of the time, he is not talking about you. You might think he is talking about you, but you might just be thinking it. But when you actually see him face to face, he will tell you the details, and then he will use Jesus as his messenger.

P: Yes. But why does that mean that Jesus has to die? That is what we started talking about, remember?

S: Because God wanted Jesus to . . . You can't talk to God unless you are in heaven, and that's when you die.

P: Aha!

S: I was just trying to say that.

P: Okay.

S: If you understood what I was saying . . . Go on.

P: Well, there is another way of saying it.

S: All right.

P: Think about love. When you love someone, you give yourself up for that someone. Now, I love you, but I can't give myself up altogether for you, because then I'd be dead and I wouldn't do you any good.

S: Here . . . listen! You made me think of something. You made me think of *The Lion, the Witch and the Wardrobe*, as a matter of fact. You know the book, right? You have a witch, and she says, "But you are making a very strange decision, because when you are dead, what is there to stop me from doing harm to this boy?" In some way, *The Lion, the Witch and the Wardrobe* is definitely based on the Bible, don't you think?

P: Definitely.

54

The Image of God

Solveig: Did we talk about what God looks like?

Poppi: We sort of touched on the matter from time to time.

S: Yes. What do you think he looks like?

P: The traditional answer is that he doesn't look like anything, that God is invisible and therefore has no appearance. But there is another answer.

S: Yes?

P: He looks like Jesus, since Jesus is . . .

S: Most people think that Jesus is the image of God.

P: Well, not most people, but Christians.

S: Right.

P: And so if he is the image of God . . .

S: Then that's what God looks like. I forget when, but one time the preacher said that God looks like anybody, that we are the image of God.

P: I think that's a very stupid thing to say.

S: Why?

P: Because Jesus is the image of God, and then we're the image of Jesus and so of God. But it doesn't work backwards so that we look like God *and* he looks like us.

S: We look like God is the correct answer. Okay. Let's change the subject.

P: You think we've exhausted that one?

S: Yes. What topics haven't we talked about? Because from time to time we go on and off different subjects.

P: And that's how we will all along wander from subject to subject.

On Christian Origins

Solveig: How did Christianity become a religion? Since Jesus was Jewish and Christianity was created after him.

Poppi: That's a question with a reasonably long answer.

S: Well, that keeps us talking.

P: When Jesus was crucified, his disciples thought, "Well, that's that. We thought he was the Messiah, but he is not." Then when they met him alive after he had died, they thought that if he had risen from the dead—or rather had been raised by God from the dead—he must truly be the Messiah of Israel, the image of God—all those things Christians now say about him. That's how it got started. To begin with, that means simply that there were Jews who believed in Jesus. Now, do you know about the temple in Jerusalem? As long as the temple was there, it was the center for Jews of all kinds. There were as many different kinds of Jews in Jesus' day as there are Protestants now—Baptists, Methodists, Lutherans, Presbyterians, and so forth. There were all kinds of different groups, but the thing that held them together was the temple, where they all came to worship.

S: Okay, but back to my question. How did there come to be so many kinds of Christian religions?

56

P: Jews, you mean.

S: No, Christians. What are the differences between them?

P: There is one big difference between Eastern and Western Christians . . .

S: Yes, but I mean the difference between Baptist, Catholic, and so on.

P: Do you know about the Reformation?

S: I think . . . Sort of.

P: In the sixteenth century, there were theologians in the church who thought the church needed to be reformed in certain respects, that it had begun teaching things and following practices that were not in accord with the true nature of Christianity. That wasn't anything unusual. That's what theologians are supposed to say. The church always somehow needs to be reformed, and the theologians are there to say so. It just happened that the reforms that these people wanted—Luther and Calvin particularly . . .

S: What does it mean to reform something?

P: It means to reshape it. It just happened that the changes that Luther and others wanted were very offensive to the people in power in the church at the time.

S: So they decided to split up.

P: The people in power in the church at the time . . .

S: Wait. They were mostly Catholic.

P: At that time, everybody considered themselves Catholic.

S: But they wouldn't have been called Catholic; they would just have been called Christian. But they would have been considered Catholic now.

P: The pope at the time, Leo the 10th, set out to shut Luther and the others up, to make them stop demanding reform.

S: What time period is that?

P: The sixteenth century.

S: So right after the Middle Ages.

P: The thing really boiled over in 1517–18.

S: Is this the time of Henry the 8th as well? Because he wanted to get divorced, and he wasn't allowed to. Well, he would have called it separating, and the church wouldn't let him, so he decided to start his own religion. Wasn't that antiestablishmentarianism also?

P: He didn't decide to start his own religion. Henry just decided that the church in England would no longer be obedient to the pope. But other than that, Henry didn't have much he wanted to change.

S: Isn't that what the word antidisestablishmentarianism means?

P: No.

S: What is antidisestablishmentarianism about then?

P: Establishmentarianism is wanting to stick to what is established.

S: Right.

P: Disestablishmentarianism is wanting to do away with whatever *is* established. Right?

S: Yes. (laughter)

P: Antidisestablishmentarianism is being opposed to those who are disestablishmentarian.

S: (much laughter)

P: And you could keep on adding prefixes as long as you wanted, I guess. But that is not to our point. Henry didn't particularly want to change the church. He just wanted to run the church instead of having the pope do it. He made himself head of the English church instead of the pope.

S: He could. But it wasn't a good thing to do.

P: I don't think so. No.

S: Well, it might have been a good thing to do, otherwise . . .

P: In England, it was just a matter of politics to begin with. Henry wanted to be head of the church to allow himself to separate from his wife.

S: Right. But he was the king, so wouldn't the pope have to listen to him?

P: Theoretically, not on this point. But practically speaking, he was the king, so he just did it.

S: Right. But that was only in England. Because, for instance, in the book *The Daughter of Venice*, this girl is growing up there, and there is still the pope.

P: What time is this?

S: Sixteenth century—or 1600s—and the pope is still there.

P: The pope is still there now.

S: Yeah, I know . . . But if she had been living in England, the pope would not have been considered the ruler of the church.

P: And he wouldn't have been considered that in Germany or Norway or Sweden or Denmark either by that time. Let me finish telling what happened.

S: Okay.

P: Pope Leo the 10th told those like Luther who were proposing reforms in the church that they had to stop. The problem was that people were so in favor of what Luther was saying that instead many stopped listening to the pope. You see how it could go either way?

S: I'm all confused now. Luther was against Henry the 8th . . .

P: Yes. They only by accident ended up rebelling against the pope at more or less the same time.

S: Okay. Because Luther didn't want that, did he?

P: It happened for very different reasons.

S: Luther wanted to change the church.

P: Only in very specific respects. Do you want me to say what they were?

S: Yes.

P: Luther thought that some of the things the church had begun to do during the Middle Ages, like indulgences, as they were called . . .

S: What do you mean?

P: I'll come back to that in a minute. Luther thought indulgences should be stopped because they gave the impression that God loves us because of what we do instead of on account of what Christ did. You see there is obviously a choice here. Why does God love us? Because we are such nice people?

S: Well, nice is not really considered an adjective.

P: Such good people then? Or because of what Christ did?

S: Neither; because he loves us.

P: That's true in a certain way.

S: He loves us; he created us and wanted us for company. Or that's what we think; we don't actually know.

P: Well, I think we do know it.

S: We don't actually know. We won't know till we are dead.

P: If it's not true, you won't know it then either, because you won't know anything.

S: True. You will just be all confused.

P: You won't even be confused; you just won't be. Now, what the Christian faith says is that Christ . . . You're quite right, God loves us because he loves us. But what Christ is, is what he does by way of loving us.

S: He gave us Christ so that . . . Wait! But Christ isn't why he loves us.

P: The answer to that is both yes and no. It's why he loves us in the sense that Christ is always with God, so whether you say that God loves us on account of Christ or that God just loves us, it comes to the same thing.

S: Okay. But what was it we were talking about before?

P: Indulgences.

S: Well, I know one thing—why Luther wouldn't approve the church.

P: Why?

S: He's been living in the Middle Ages. And it was more or less be good all your life, because they had all those gargoyles to scare people and to make them good. They should just be good because they are good, not because they are afraid not to be.

P: That last is true. On the other hand, Luther didn't mind the gargoyles much; he thought they were quite cute.

S: But they are not exactly the right way to get people to be good. You should be good because you are good, not because those grotesques are telling you to.

P: Okay.

Indulgences and What Followed

Solveig: Keep going.

Poppi: About indulgences?

S: Yes.

P: This will again require a lengthy discussion. Okay?

S: Then we have to get back to our first conversation about the religions.

P: Let's finish off indulgences. There was and still is a sacrament of the church called penance. In the Protestant church now, we don't see much of it. But you know how in the church we confess our sins and the minister forgives them? In the Middle Ages, the way this worked was that you confessed your sins to the priest, one at a time.

S: Did people do it out loud or go into those little box thingies? Confessionals?

P: In the little boxes *and* out loud.

S: In the confessionals with the priest on one side and you on the other?

P: They didn't actually have those boxes in the Middle Ages, but it worked the same way.

S: Did they go into a special room?

P: Yes. Then after confession, the priest forgives you.

S: Hopefully. And didn't he also say, "I won't tell any-one"?

P: That wasn't part of the ritual, but he was sworn not to tell. That's still true now. People confess to me, and I'm sworn not to ever tell anyone what they say.

S: They do? You won't even tell me?

P: No, of course not.

S: But what if someone said, "I want to murder a person?" Wouldn't they still tell?

P: Not unless the priest thinks the person *is* going to murder someone else. If someone confesses to me that he is thinking of murdering someone, and I believe him, *that* I can tell to the police. But we're way off the subject. First the confession, then the forgiveness, and then the priest would say, "Now, by way of showing that you reallly mean you are sorry, you're going to do something special." If it was really serious, perhaps make a pilgrimage. You know what a pilgrimage is?

S: Yes. It would be traveling from church to church, worshiping.

P: If it was something really trivial . . .

S: Like what?

P: "I was nasty to my Poppi yesterday." (laughter) "I refused to eat with a fork." Something like that. (laughter) Then it would only be a couple of extra prayers that you wouldn't ordinarily say. "When you go to bed, don't just say, 'God bless Mommy, Daddy, and so on,' but also say the Lord's Prayer." It could be something big or something small, but the point of doing it was to show that you were sorry and planned not to do it again.

S: Or would you have to pay the church?

P: We're coming to that. Supposing you are the penitent, and I'm the priest, and . . .

S: "Father, please forgive me."

P: And I say, "But to show you really mean it, you have to attend church twice this week."

S: No! (laughter)

P: And you don't do it. Where are we then? You are in debt to the church.

S: It's sort of like if you want to borrow money from the bank, and you didn't pay it back.

P: You owe them.

S: Right.

P: Now, somebody had the bright idea of allowing debts to the church to be paid off with money. What I really owe the church is a pilgrimage . . .

S: But that's what you don't want to do.

P: So what I do is I contribute for an indulgence. The church indulges me.

S: That's not a very good idea, I don't think.

P: Luther didn't think so either.

S: Which is why the whole thing got started. What's the point in paying the church? They could use the money, but there's really no point in doing it.

P: But the reason Luther objected was it gives the impression . . .

S: That the church wants money.

P: That's true too.

S: If you just pay money, it's like, "Oh, yeah, I'll just pay money for love," but you don't actually love someone.

P: It gives the impression that I can buy God's love. Now, the church never meant that, but it does give that impression. So Luther said, "You have to stop selling indulgences," and the pope said, "We can't stop."

S: I don't like this pope.

P: He wasn't a very good pope, and no one, Catholic or Protestant, really thinks he was. Although that pope was a *very* good one in the matter of art.

S: What do you mean?

P: He was the one who pushed the building of St. Peter's.

S: Well, that is okay then.

P: Some of the great works of the Renaissance were commissioned by that pope. But as a leader of the Christian church, he was pretty much a bust—and most people agree to that.

S: As well as me.

P: The pope put Luther and anybody who followed him under the ban. That meant that they weren't allowed to speak on theological matters; they weren't even supposed to attend church.

S: I wouldn't tell someone not to go to church. That's ridiculous.

P: You would if you were trying to make him quiet. Luther by that time had started to be famous.

S: People were beginning to like his ideas.

P: Yes. And the printing press had just been invented . . .

S: So wasn't he really holding him for ransom?

P: No.

S: So they couldn't buy him back exactly like they could with everything else?

P: No. Printing had just been invented, so for the first time there was something like newspapers. And the printers all over Europe carried the story of Luther.

S: This was right after Wartburg.

P: Right.

S: Or during Wartburg, and he made the first Bible and the first book.

P: Well, it wasn't the first Bible, but the first printed in German.

S: Right. I said it was the first *book*. The first Bibles were made by monks.

P: So then people all over had the choice: were they going to listen to Luther or the pope? And most people in Germany and lots of people elsewhere, in Norway and Sweden and Denmark, in Finland, Poland, northern Italy, in northern Spain and parts of France . . .

S: They all said Luther! So what did the pope do?

P: He banned them from the church.

S: They could start their own churches. And by the way, they could still pray in their own homes.

P: Well, that's not how Christians do it. They pray in their homes, but first of all they pray together around the bread and the wine at the Eucharist.

S: Yes, but if you have to, you can just pray in your own home. It's fine.

P: If you *have* to.

Church Divisions

Solveig: This pope may have been very smart in the matter of the arts, but he was not smart in the matter of corrections.

Poppi: Probably true. And he certainly was not a very good theologian. Now, the problem was that once the church split like this, the part that didn't anymore obey the pope kept on splitting. Once you found out you could split, everybody who had a different idea about how to reform the church started a new church.

S: So you can say Luther started all this church-splitting.

P: Or you can say Leo the 10th did.

S: Right. But I'm saying . . . Luther started which religion exactly? I mean which part of Christianity?

P: We usually refer to everyone who is not Catholic as Protestant. The part of Protestanism that followed Luther most closely is called Lutheran. Your Mimi and I are Lutherans.

S: Luther started the Lutherans; but who started the Episcopalians?

P: Henry the 8th. We've already talked about that.

S: Who started the Baptists?

P: In this country, the first Baptists were Puritans. Do you remember the Puritans? Do you know how the United States got settled?

S: Yes.

P: Puritans baptized babies, but there were some Puritans who thought . . .

S: How did they get the name Baptist? Was that from John the Baptist?

P: No. Nothing to do with that. There were some Puritans who thought you shouldn't baptize people until they were old enough to choose for themselves. Like your daddy was baptized when he was grown up; he chose for himself.

S: His family is Jewish, though.

P: Lots of people get baptized as adults. And some Puritans thought everybody should do it that way and that people who had been baptized as babies really should do it over again.

S: Why was that?

P: Because they didn't think baptism done when people were babies and couldn't speak for themselves really counted. So they baptized them over again. In the matter of how they got to be called Baptists, baptist is short for anabaptist; and in Latin, *ana-* means over again.

S: What other Christians are there?

P: Well, there are Reformed . . . They are a broad branch that includes Presbyterians. You've heard of them?

S: Isn't Wallace[3] Presbyterian?

P: Yes. Lots of the Christians in Princeton are Presbyterian.

S: Except us.

P: I'm sort of half Anglican and half Lutheran. You are an Episcopalian. The Reformed are Presbyterians, Congregationalists, German Reformed, Dutch Reformed, and so on. They are all alike in one respect—that is, that the other great reformer, John Calvin, is their theological founder.

S: I've heard that name . . . How are Quakers considered?

P: Quakers started as Christians.

S: But they don't believe that Jesus is the Son of God.

P: Well, some do and some don't.

S: They believe he was a good person but not that he was the Son of God.

P: Some do and some don't. Some Quakers are Christian and some aren't. But you know why they were originally called Quakers?

S: Why?

P: Because they quaked. They were so excited when they prayed that they would shake.

S: (laughter) Oh dear!

P: And we called them Quakers, meaning people who quaked. They have calmed down considerably since they

3. The director of the Center of Theological Inquiry where Poppi works, and a favorite of Solveig's.

70

started. They may be the calmest people around right now.

S: Good.

P: There are Methodists. These are people who think that John Wesley and Charles Wesley had the truest interpretation of Protestantism. There are . . .

S: Okay. So now we can get back to our original conversation again.

P: And that was . . . Oh, we *are* back to it. The original question was, How did there get to be so many kinds of Protestants?

On Christian Origins Again

Solveig: That wasn't the original question. Our original question was, How did Christianity get started?

Poppi: Put it this way—of all the different kinds of Jews there were at Jesus's time, there were only two groups that could get along without the temple.

S: And those were . . .

P: And those were the people who later were called Christians, and . . .

S: Because they believed in Jesus, and all the other Jews believe that the Messiah is still to come.

P: Many kinds of Jews just disappeared when the temple was gone. But the other group of Jews that could get along without the temple were the Pharisees—you remember hearing about them.

S: I think so.

P: The Pharisees were those who thought that the very heart of Judaism was reading and obeying the Torah, the advice for a good life that is in the Old Testament. And you can take the Old Testament around with you wherever you go. You don't need a temple for that.

S: Most Bibles include the Old Testament, because we still believe the Old Testament; it's just that we believe that the Messiah has already come.

P: Right.

S: And will come back.

P: Right. That means that for Christians, Christ is the center of things; for the Pharisees, the Torah.

S: Pharisees?

P: They are mentioned in the New Testament. Jesus was always having arguments with them. Remember?

S: Sort of . . . Yes.

P: The view of the Pharisees was that you could regulate the whole of your life by the laws contained in the Old Testament. So just as the Christians could get along without the temple because they had Christ, the Pharisees could get along without the temple because they had the Old Testament. So those two kinds of Judaism survived—the Jews who believed in Jesus, and those who followed the Pharisees. What we call Judaism today is Pharisaic Judaism.

S: Okay. Let's change the conversation, because we have covered this as much as we can. Let's pick a new topic now.

Some Metaphysics

Poppi: Could God make two and two equal five?

Solveig: He couldn't, but . . . Okay, here's the thing. When mathematics were started, two plus two always equalled four, so . . . as we were talking about before, that God makes things happen but he doesn't know when it's going to happen or how it's going to happen, so he knew that two plus two was probably going to equal four.

P: Probably or certainly?

S: Certainly.

P: Okay.

S: So if two plus two equals four, then he can't just change it to two plus two equals five. He can't change his mind. Or he can change his mind, but he can't make us change his mind.

P: This is an interesting theological question to which you gave a very interesting answer. You might call it a judicious answer. What God knows is true. You can say that?

S: Right.

P: But does God know it because it is true, or is it true because God knows it?

S: Both.

P: Why?

S: Two plus two is four is true because God knows it, and he knows it because it is true. I was putting it the opposite way because if God knows it is true because it is true, he knows *that* it is true because it *is* true. But he also knows that it is true because he knows it.

P: Okay. I think that is probably right, and that is the most judicious answer.

The Resurrection and Angels

Poppi: In the Gospels, there are two kinds of stories about Jesus's resurrection: there are stories about people meeting him after he was crucified, and recognizing that he is alive, and there are stories about people going to his tomb and finding it empty. Which of these is most important?

Solveig: First, I'll tell the story. Jesus was crucified, and he was put in his tomb. Mary then came to his tomb to pray, and she found it open and there was no body inside, only an angel saying, "He is resurrected." So she goes back and tells the disciples that Jesus is resurrected, and they, of course, don't believe her. Well, they sort of believe her. Then some of the disciples go off to the tomb and do find it empty and come back. *Now* you ask the question.

P: Okay. Finding the tomb empty or meeting him alive—which do you think is most important?

S: Finding the tomb empty.

P: Why?

S: This doesn't have anything to do with it, but real answers in life are always strange; this one also. So . . . if Mary hadn't found the tomb open and empty, the disciples wouldn't have been ready for Jesus to come; they wouldn't have been prepared. And I think Jesus was also a part of this; he wanted to be sure they were ready. If they wouldn't have found the tomb empty and believed it, he would have probably just stayed there and waited, whereas because they found the tomb empty, they were ready for him, so Jesus could come.

P: I would say that it is the opposite.

S: Why?

P: Finding the tomb empty could just mean that somebody had stolen the body . . .

S: Whereas actually running into Jesus shows that he is alive. But here's the thing! The part of the angels is the most important part in the resurrection. It is sort of hidden there, unless you totally think about it. The angel is so very important, but it is strange. The angel told Mary—and Mary has had this strange connection with angels for quite a long time, of course, because the angel came to her before Jesus was born . . .

P: It's not the same Mary, you know.

75

S: What?

P: The Mary who goes to the tomb is not Jesus's mother; it is Mary Magdalene.

S: Wait . . . I know, I know, I know . . . Well, Mary Magdalene had said . . .

P: I wish you were right, because it's a really cool idea.

S: Well, the angel is such a very important part in this story, nevertheless. If Mary hadn't heard the angel say, "Jesus is alive," they wouldn't have been ready in the first place. They wouldn't have believed her if the angel hadn't told her. In some ways, I think the angels are the hidden most important characters in the Bible.

P: All along or just at this point?

S: In most of it.

P: Really?

S: Yes.

P: Like where and when and why?

S: Jesus's birth—the angel is the one who told Mary. When you just read it quickly through, you think Mary is the most important part of the story, but that's not true. She wouldn't have known that Jesus was the Son of God if the angel hadn't told her, and then she wouldn't have believed it if the angel hadn't told her. And Mary Magdalene might not have believed either if the angel wasn't there. And then there are so many other stories where the angels are important.

Angels, the Spirit, and Our Minds

Poppi: What do you think an angel is?

Solveig: You want to know what *I* think?

P: That's what I asked.

S: Well, people normally say angels are good people who have died.

P: The Bible doesn't say that at all.

S: No. *People* say that. Angels are parts of God, but they are also the good in people. They are the Holy Spirit. They bring out the good in people, all the wonderful things that God has created in you. You may be a horrible person, but the angels are the ones who can bring out the good in you.

P: In the Bible, the angels and the Holy Spirit are two different things.

S: But the angels are so important. (a big sigh) You don't understand.

P: I think I do, and I even agree with you about the importance of the angels in the Bible. But they are not the Holy Spirit.

S: No, I'm not saying they are the Holy Spirit; the angels may not be the Holy Spirit, but they bring out the good in people. They really do, because they are what makes you believe. They may not be the Holy Spirit . . . But they are the *image* of the Holy Spirit. The Spirit cannot be seen; the angels are the messengers for the Holy Spirit, in some way.

P: Do you know what the word angel means?

S: No.

P: It means messenger.

S: God's messengers and the Holy Spirit's messengers . . . See, it works both ways.

P: In Hebrew, it's *melech*; in Greek, it's *angelos*; and both mean messenger.

S: That's good. So in some ways, I'm correct.

P: They are messengers of God, and if you want to say of the Holy Spirit, I think that's okay too.

S: Because the Holy Spirit doesn't have any form or body; the Holy Spirit is a spirit. I just thought of something—it's very strange.

P: What?

S: The dead people—they may be dead, but that doesn't mean they have no feelings. The Holy Spirit maybe takes their feeling in some way but lets them have their feelings. And the Holy Spirit helps others with those feelings. Does that make any sense to you?

P: Not a lot. But I can sort of revise it to make sense and see if that's what you mean.

S: Okay.

P: In the creed that we say on Sundays, in the third article, we first say we believe in the Holy Spirit, then there is a list of things we say that follow from that.

S: Of course. Here's the thing. We wouldn't believe in God if it weren't for the Holy Spirit. Does that make any sense?

P: Yes.

S: We wouldn't believe if it weren't for the Holy Spirit. The Holy Spirit gives us our emotions, feelings, the senses—smell, sight, taste . . .

P: Does the Holy Spirit give us our physical senses?

S: Yes.

P: You think so?

S: Our brains, for instance. The Holy Spirit gives us not only the feelings in our heart but in our brain. And those feelings help us with our sight, taste, smell, hearing—what's the other one?

P: Touch.

S: Right. Because our brain is what gives us those feelings, and the Holy Spirit is what gives us our brain.

P: But you have told me that you don't owe your mathematical skills or your reading ability . . .

S: No. Here's the thing. You don't owe it to *religion*, but the Holy Spirit isn't religion. Or it's religion in the sense that everybody shares it. The Holy Spirit can be shared by anyone of any religion because the Holy Spirit is spirit.

P: That contradicts what you once said about baptism.

S: What do you mean?

P: I once asked what happens when you are baptized, and you said that you get the Holy Spirit.

S: Yes . . .

P: Well, if you already have the Holy Spirit, that doesn't make any sense.

S: Okay. You don't have the Holy Spirit. In some ways you have to . . . Everybody has the Spirit when they are born, but the Holy Spirit gives a feeling that we didn't have when we were born.

P: It changes our feelings?

S: Right. When you are born, you may think—of course, you don't have much thought except, "I want milk," and, "Mama come to me," and things like that—but before you are baptized, you might think, "I like that person," but when you have the Holy Spirit, you would think of it in a much more emotional, interesting way.

P: I'll go along with that.

S: The Holy Spirit—Jews have it and other religions too.

P: I don't think that is *quite* right.

S: They have it in a sense, but it is not strong until you are baptized.

P: Let's put it this way—the Spirit is *active* everywhere, but *having* the Holy Spirit is something a little different.

S: Right. The Holy Spirit is active everywhere, but if you don't have it, you have to do certain things. But here's the thing—Jews do have it because they believe in God too. In all religions, they don't believe in different things. Do you understand?

P: I understand. I think you have basically the right ideas, but they are getting a little . . .

S: Mixed up from what I said before. Yes, I know. Anyway, what else?

David and Solomon

Poppi: Do you want to tell the King David story?

Solveig: Yes. King David was a shepherd, and he had many brothers. When King David was young, he wasn't like his brothers. His brothers were strong and mighty, and his father loved his brothers, but he didn't love David half as much because he didn't have strength like his brothers. Then one day a prophet came.

P: Do you remember the prophet's name?

S: Samuel. So David was out with the sheep, and the prophet came, and he asked for all the sons to come. So they all came except David, because his father thought, "What's the point? Why would he want David in the first place?" But the prophet kept saying, "No. Not that one. No. Not that one." So the father decided to bring in David. And the prophet said, "This one. You are to be the rightful king over this land." So there were the Philistines who were against the Israelites, and they had a giant on their side called Goliath. The Philistines hated the Israelites, and so they started attacking them. And all of David's brothers went to war against the Philistines and Goliath. Nobody could defeat Goliath, so David went with his slingshot, and he went over to Goliath, and Goliath said, "Does anybody challenge me?" And David said, "I do." And Goliath said, "You're such a little boy you could never win against me," and David said, "I have God on my side." So David takes his slingshot, puts a rock in it, and hits Goliath right in the center of his forehead and knocks Goliath out. Then with Goliath's own sword, David cuts off Goliath's head. So then everybody says, "Hurrah, hurrah, hurrah!" So David is taken to become king, because the old king, Saul, had been killed during the battle.

P: Not that same battle.

S: No, but a different one. Then David became king, unlike Saul's own son.

P: Jonathan.

S: David and Jonathan were very, very good friends, but David was going to become king and that was that. Well, actually there is a little flaw in that. After he had become king, he was looking out his window one day, and he saw a woman bathing on her balcony, and the woman's name was Bathsheba, and he wanted to know her name. David asked the servants to have Bathsheba come over. You must remember that David has been married to many women before.

P: Not serially, but to many at once. That is called a harem.

S: Yes. Like in *The King and I*. And the servants tell David that Bathsheba is married to one of his men. So David tells his servants to take the knight to one of the fiercest battles but not to tell the knight, so he is taken to the fiercest of battles and he dies. Then Bathsheba is taken to David, and David had wanted this all along. And Bathsheba probably knew that something like this had happened, because if I were her, I would probably find it quite odd if one day my husband were sent to King David and the next day he was dead. Probably that is what she was thinking, but she . . . Now, here's the thing . . . Now you tell the rest of the story.

P: The Nathan story.

S: Because you tell it so well.

P: After this had happened, Nathan the prophet came to David and said, "I want to tell you a story: Once upon a time, there was a rich man who had many, many sheep, and there was a poor man who had just one sheep. The rich man couldn't abide that there should be even one sheep that he didn't have, so he sent and took the one sheep from the poor man and put it in his flock. King David, you are so wise—what should be done to that rich man?" And David said, "He should be killed for this terrible crime." Then Nathan said, "*You* are the rich man. You had a whole harem of wives and concubines, and you had to have the one wife of your knight."

S: And so?

P: So David repented in sackcloth and ashes. Things never went quite right for David after that. Bathsheba became the mother of the next king of Israel. Do you remember what his name was?

S: Hmm . . .

P: You don't know? The greatest of all the kings . . . Solomon.

S: Oh yes. I do know. Now tell me . . .

P: Solomon made Israel into a small empire. He took David's capital city, Jerusalem, and made glorious palaces and a wall around it and made it a great city. He had a powerful army. He traded far and wide. His caravans went out all over the known world. When he became king, the Lord asked him what he would like to have, and Solomon said, "Above all, I would like wisdom to govern this people well." And the Lord said, "That was a very wise choice in itself. And you will be wise."

S: Wait, I'm all confused . . .

P: On the other hand . . .

S: Retell the whole story, because I'm confused.

P: Okay. Solomon was David's son and Bathsheba's. When he became king, he asked the Lord for a gift. The Lord said, "What would you like?" And Solomon said, "I would like to be wise so that I will be able to rule this kingdom well." And the Lord said, "That was itself a very wise choice. And you will be wise." So from one point of view, Solomon was the greatest of the kings of Israel, a wise king who governed well. He made David's city, Jerusalem, into a powerful city with palaces and walls.

S: What else could he have done?

P: What else could he have asked for from the Lord?

S: Well, he could have asked something for his *people*, because he seems to already be wise. He could have asked for his people to be well. Or he could have asked for peace throughout the whole world for the rest of time.

P: No ancient king would have thought of asking that, because making war was a big part of what they did, and Solomon had a powerful army.

S: Then he was not very wise.

P: That's a possible argument.

S: I like arguments.

P: Solomon also did one extremely important thing besides building up the nation. He built the temple, the place where Israel came to meet the Lord.

The Land of Israel

Solveig: Now what do you want to talk about?

Poppi: We haven't finished with Solomon.

S: We haven't?

P: We've only looked at the good side of Solomon; the bad side is the following: All of this cost a great deal of money, and Solomon pretty well bankrupted the country with taxes, so that when Solomon died, half of Israel revolted against Solomon's policies and would not have Solomon's son for their king. So Solomon was the last king to rule over the whole of Israel. From then on, there were two countries, each with their king. The one in the north was called Israel, and the one in the south was called Judah.

S: Okay. Now I've another question. How was Palestine created? 'Cause for many years, Israel and Palestine . . .

P: When the Israelite tribes came into the part of the world that we call Palestine, obviously there were already people living there. The Israelites conquered the land.

S: But weren't they there first? The Israelites?

P: No. Remember, they had been captives in Egypt?

S: Right.

P: They escaped from captivity in Egypt, then came through the desert, and then they came into Palestine. Now, there were people living there when they came, so they had to conquer the land. Then for the most part, they absorbed the population into Israel, with marriages and so on. That part of the world remained the possession of the Israelites for a thousand years. Then when the Roman Empire destroyed the temple, finally and permanently, there was a time when it was sort of a no-man's-land. There was a population, obviously, but it wasn't anything in particular. Then it became Christian as the Christian church grew. So for five hundred years, Palestine was a Christian country. Then in the seventh century, the Arabs, coming from Arabia, conquered it, and it became an Arab country for more hundreds of years.

S: And then . . .

P: And then many Jews came back.

S: "We want our land!"

P: The United Nations passed a resolution dividing the country. Two-thirds of it would be Arab and one-third Israel.

S: And when was that?

P: 1948. But the surrounding Arab nations—Syria, Jordan, Egypt—were not willing for there to be an Israeli state at all, so their armies immediately attacked. The very day the state of Israel was proclaimed in accordance with the U.N. resolution, the Arab nations attacked. To everybody's astonishment, in the fighting that followed, the Jews won, so that the part of Palestine that is Israel became larger than the United Nations had originally proposed. And more or less the same thing has happened twice since. Twice since, the Arab armies have attacked, and twice since, they have lost, and each time, Israel got to be bigger. Who really owns all that is hard to say. If you go according to who lived there the longest, it's clearly the Jews.

S: It goes to who has been there first.

P: If you say it belongs to who was there first, then it was the people who were living there when Israel came. But no one knows who they are now.

S: Well, they're very complicated, these people and this land.

Santa Claus and Other Saints

Poppi: Okay. What do you want to talk about?
Solveig: Let's talk about Christmas.
P: What would you like to ask about Christmas?

87

S: Well . . . how did Santa become a part of Christmas?

P: That's a long story. Would you like to hear it?

S: Yes. And I have an idea about something.

P: There was a real saint, a bishop in—I think—the fourth century who was called Nicholas. He became famous and saintly because of his kindness to people, so St. Nicholas became the patron saint of gift-giving. Now, in Dutch, St. Nicholas is *Sinter Klas*, and it was the Dutch who settled in New York—which was once called New Amsterdam—who brought the story of *Sinter Klas* to this country.

S: Here's the thing. We think of Santa Claus now as this jolly old person who brings gifts to children—and grownups too. Now, in a way, Santa Claus—because there is no Santa Claus—is not a real person; he's a spirit. He's sort of like the spirit of Christmas.

P: He's not exactly the spirit of real Christmas . . .

S: Right, it's so strange. It's not like he comes down the chimney and puts gifts in your stocking.

P: Christians have a lot of saints, people who are remembered for having been particularly good, in one way or another. Now, whatever you think of this jolly old man in the red suit who comes down the chimney, there is in fact a St. Nicholas.

S: There is. But there is really no one who comes down the chimney and puts things . . .

P: No. Of course not, and you know that. Did you ever think there was?

S: Yes.

P: You did?

S: When I was little.

P: What made you change your mind?

S: For a while I thought about it . . . Well, actually the first reason I thought about it was either the Easter bunny or the tooth fairy. And then I thought, if *that* is not real . . . Then I kept asking Mommy to tell me, and finally I said, "Please, please tell me!" and then we had a long discussion in the bathroom in our apartment. We were talking, and I brought up Santa Claus—I don't really know why we had a serious conversation. I asked her, "Santa Claus cannot be real, can he?" Actually, all this started when I was in bed one day, and I woke up in the middle of the night, and I called for Mommy and I asked her, "Is Santa Claus real?" And she wouldn't say anything. Then years later, I asked her one night and she told me, "It's not that he is a real man who comes down your chimney and puts presents in your stockings. He is kind of a jolly thing that represents Christmas."

P: Well, he represents the gift-giving side of Christmas— and the gift-getting side of Christmas. Which, of course, isn't the main point of Christmas at all.

S: Of course, the main part of Christmas is Jesus's being born, but then everyone kept adding things to it. If Jesus could be an old peasant man you met on the street, he could definitely be the person you're giving a present to.

P: Well, you know what Jesus said once . . .

S: He was part of everything.

P: He's not *part* of everybody. But you know what he did say once . . .

S: What?

P: Anyone who gives a present to someone who really needs it—which wouldn't include you or me, by the way . . .

S: Of course not. All right . . .

P: If anyone gives a present to someone who really needs it, it is as if he had given it to me. Now, that means when, for example, you see the Salvation Army out on the streets before Christmas, with a guy in a Santa Claus outfit asking for donations, that *is* a little like giving a present to Jesus, because that money goes to buy things for people who really need it—to buy a good dinner for people on Christmas Day who otherwise wouldn't have it, to pay for shelters for people who don't have homes . . .

S: But how do you suppose it got started that Santa Claus would come down the chimney and give presents in your stocking?

P: Because one guy wrote a poem. The *Sinter Klas* legend—that first was Dutch and then came to New York, lived on there, and then this man—I don't remember his name now—wrote a poem . . .

S: "'Twas the night before Christmas, and all through the house not a creature was stirring, not even a mouse."

P: He wrote the poem, and he made up the business . . .

S: He made up the whole thing?

P: He made up the business about Santa Claus coming on a sleigh . . .

S: I never imagined . . . When did he live?

P: Nineteenth century. But that's all I can remember.

S: You mean before that, nobody . . .

P: Nobody thought about Santa coming on a sleigh or down the chimney. And people got so much fun out of the poem that . . .

S: They started making it real.

P: The funny part is that his poem . . .

S: Caused people to start putting stockings up.

P: Replaced the original story about the good bishop who gave presents to people.

S: So then we have the jolly old man.

P: Let me say something, Sol . . .

S: Yes?

P: There is a real saint named St. Nicholas.

S: Yes. Of course.

P: And it would be much more in keeping with the meaning of Christmas if we remembered the good St. Nicholas.

S: You see, most people, those who don't go to church, mostly think of Christmas as getting presents, and most people don't even think about the real reason we're celebrating it.

P: Well, that's been true for a long time now. But to go back to the matter of saints . . . Many Christians will ask saints to pray for them, like I can ask you to pray for me.

S: But I'm not a saint.

P: You don't have to be. Anybody can pray for somebody else. Right? Well, one of the ideas about saints is that people we are pretty sure really are saints, like St. Nicholas, are surely with God, so that you can ask them to pray for you. You could have a prayer like this: "Dear St. Nicholas, please pray to God to make me less acquisitive at Christmastime and more interested in people who really need gifts."

S: I guess that would be a good thing, but you know some people only think about themselves at Christmas.

P: You don't want to be one of those, I trust?

S: No.

P: So that would be a good prayer to try sometime: "Dear St. Nicholas, ask God to make me less selfish."

S: Amen.

P: Amen.

Calendars and Ritual

Solveig: Let's talk about Advent. How did Advent become a big thing that everybody does?

Poppi: It isn't a big thing that most people do.

S: Well, I mean that Christians do.

P: Not even all Christians make much out of it. It's those who keep what is called the church calendar. Do you know what that is?

S: What?

P: The church has its own calendar. The church's New Year's Day is the first Sunday of Advent. Then there are Sundays in Advent, then Christmas, then Epiphany on January the 6th, then there are some Sundays after Epiphany, then there is Lent, which is forty-days long, then there is Holy Week . . .

S: Yes, but why . . .

P: People have a need to have a calendar, to know where they are in the year.

S: But you also need to prepare.

P: That's right. There are two big seasons for preparing in the church year. One is Advent, preparing for Christmas, and the other is Lent, preparing for Holy Week.

S: Right.

P: But there is another thing. What does the word Advent mean?

S: I don't . . . "Ad-vent"—it means to add the vent. (laughter)

P: It's Latin. *Ad* is a preposition—here a prefix, rather— and it means toward something. And *venire* means to come. So Advent is the season of the year toward Christ's coming.

S: Yes. But why are we looking forward to Christ's death?

P: That's in Lent.

S: Right, that's what I'm talking about. Why are we looking forward to his death?

P: Because it isn't just his death; we are looking forward at the same time to his death and resurrection. That's Holy Week, starting with Palm Sunday, and then Holy Thursday with foot washing and all . . .

S: Maunday Thursday.

P: And then Good Friday and Saturday night and Sunday morning of Easter. That's the main act of the whole church year.

S: Yes, and my favorite of all. My favorite parts are Easter and Christmas. Christmas you get to go caroling; and Easter, the cathedral is all decorated—it's so much fun.

P: But it is no good having Easter without Good Friday.

S: Yeah, I know. Maunday Thursday is pretty fun at the cathedral, when the choristers go running out.

P: Why do they do that?

S: Maybe to show that they are so upset or something. I don't know.

P: You remember what happened. Jesus was crucified on Friday. The night before—Thursday—Jesus had supper with his disciples.

S: Correct.

P: He got arrested and all of his disciples fled.

S: So the chorus is sort of like the disciples.

P: That's right, they run away.

S: But why the choristers?

P: Because they are the ones singing. You could have the whole congregation run out, but that would be sort of a mess.

S: Why do they take the lamps down?

P: At the end of Thursday service, you get the cathedral ready for Friday.

S: Right.

P: And on Good Friday, there aren't any lights. There is nothing on the altar—the whole place has been stripped bare. Now, at the cathedral, they have those great lamps, and to turn them off, they have to let them down. The other lights they just extinguish—the candles and so forth.

S: How do they light those lamps?

P: With a candle, the way they light the other candles.

S: Why do they let them down?

P: It's more dramatic. The reason they come down at all is so they can turn them off.

S: This is sort of out of order in this part, but what is the purpose of Ash Wednesday?

P: It's the beginning of Lent. It's on a Wednesday in the middle of a week—you have to be able to count forty days . . .

S: (singing) "Forty days and forty nights . . ."

P: Because it was forty days that Jesus spent in the wilderness being tempted. So Lent starts forty days before the first day of Holy Week. And the ashes . . . Do you know where they get those ashes? They burn the palms from last year's Palm Sunday.

S: From last year?

P: Yes. The palms that everybody waves . . .

S: But how do they have enough? Lots of people take them home.

P: There is plenty left over.

S: Where do they burn them?

P: That depends on the church; any place will do. You mix the ashes with a little oil so that they aren't just powder, so that they stick to your finger and so that you can make a mark.

S: In the shape of a cross. Well, it's supposed to be shaped like that, but by the next day, it's not going to look like that.

P: Do you know why they do it on your forehead? Because when you are baptized, you're anointed with oil in the same place.

S: Did I cry when I was baptized?

P: No.

S: Was I a good little baby?

P: You were a rambunctious baby, as I recall—this is not surprising. But you didn't cry. There were quite a few babies and others being baptized when you were, and many of them were not well behaved.

S: I was the best behaved of them. Of course, I'm always the best.

P: You know, a lot of this when you are just praising your-self isn't going into the book.[4]

S: I know. We talked about the purpose of baptism. Let's think of something else. Palm Sunday is pretty obvious. Okay . . . how come the priests have their own special chairs if we're all supposed to be equal?

P: There is a problem about that. In one way, we're all supposed to be equal; on the other hand, not everybody celebrates the Lord's Supper. Priests are ordained to celebrate the Lord's Supper. That means they have to sit close to the altar, so you keep reserved places for them.

S: Well, of course. But why don't they sit in the same chairs as everybody else does? Except for people who need high-backed chairs . . .

P: A lot of Christians think they should.

S: I don't think they should. I'm just wondering why.

P: If you go to a Presbyterian church, they have ordinary chairs for the clergy.

S: I was just wondering. I don't really care either way. It actually makes the cathedral prettier.

P: In the ancient church, the ceremonial garments, the fancy dress of the leaders of the church, came to be like the leaders of the empire, so if you have a throne for the emperor, you have a throne for the bishop.

4. But as you see, some of it did.

S: Here's my other question: How come in the Middle Ages the priest would have that special kind of haircut? Was it to make a halo?

P: No.

S: Because it does look like a halo.

P: I know, but the reason is to show humility. Long flowing hair was what worldly people wore.

S: Like duchesses and kings and queens . . .

P: And just ordinary folk if they had a little money. Monks and friars cut off almost all their hair as a sign that they were poor, that they didn't have any money of their own, which they didn't.

S: But they were rich at heart, whereas many who had long hair were rich in money but poor in heart.

P: That was indeed the idea.

S: What about the cause for gargoyles and grotesques? They were supposed to show that you should behave well; otherwise you'd have these creatures . . .

P: I don't know if that is true.

S: Well, that's what I was told at school.

P: Maybe so. My guess would be a simpler one: people *like* to make up these funny animals. You remember the exhibit we saw yesterday? There were snakes, gorgons . . .

S: Yes, but weren't they supposed to show that is what you would have if you were going to be in hell?

P: I don't think so. In the Middle Ages, the cathedral or the church was the only really big fancy building in town.

So all the artistic impulse of the people went into the making of the church, and in places where it really didn't count, they liked making these funny animals for the same reason they always have.

S: Just for the enjoyment. But why on churches, then?

P: Because that is the only place they had to do it.

S: I don't know if you are right, though. Because many a book has said that was the cause for it, and my teacher has been teaching about the Middle Ages for twelve years.

P: Well, she may be right, but my opinion would be that there is a much simpler explanation. A lot of those grotesques—for example, in the great cathedrals of France—are not frightening, just cute.

Trinitarian and Incarnational Matters

Solveig: A new subject—the Virgin Mary. Who was she besides the mother of Jesus?

Poppi: We know very little for sure. According to the New Testament, she was a young woman in Nazareth engaged to a man named Joseph . . .

S: Who had God speak to her.

P: And that's all we know. But later, people told whole biographies. How much of this has been remembered and how much is just made up is very hard to say.

S: Are there any other interesting subjects?

P: Well, there is one that you brought up earlier about Santa Claus.

S: I did . . . that Santa Claus is like the Holy Spirit.

P: Well, that's wrong.

S: Right.

P: That's what I wanted to talk about. Look, there are all kinds of spirits. Everybody has a spirit. You're very spirited.

S: Of course everybody has to have spirit.

P: But some people don't have much. Some people are kind of *dis*pirited.

S: In the way you think of Santa Claus—not the Dutch Santa Claus—he is sort of like a messenger from the Holy Spirit—in a way.

P: Ahh . . .

S: Because he is the spirit of Christmas, not including Jesus, of course.

P: Now, let me teach a little. Not only individual people but groups of people like a football team or like a class have each of them a spirit, which is two things. One, it's the character of that person or group. But two, it's the character of that person or group insofar as that character goes out from that person to affect other people. When you're around me, your liveliness—your character—impacts me. Right?

S: Like my pulling your beard.

P: Absolutely. So that God has a Spirit means that God doesn't stay shut up in himself . . .

S: I would hope not.

P: But that the goodness and mercy—and wrath, when it comes to that—that is in God blows out from him to hit you and me. And that means that just like your spirit is yours and not mine, even though your spirit affects me, so God's Spirit is his and not a spirit like Santa Claus.

S: But then God *is* a spirit. He doesn't *need* a spirit. It's not like you are given a spirit; he already is spirit. He doesn't get the spirit; he's born with spirit. He *is* spirit.

P: Right.

S: Right. It's hard to explain the meanings of God, I must say.

P: You think so?

S: Yes.

P: Well, yes and no. Yes, of course it's hard, but you can think of the difference   you just did—between having a spirit although you are something else, and being one.

S: You see, God and the Holy Spirit . . . The Holy Spirit is its own self in the way it comes to God too. It's God is the spirit that has the Holy Spirit.

P: God is the spirit that he has.

S: Right, and the Holy Spirit then . . .

P: Is that spirit that God has that he is.

S: Right. Well, everyone is part of God . . .

P: No.

S: Not exactly that, but every move that you do, God is watching. I wonder how it can see.

P: It isn't an it.

S: What is it?

P: He.

S: He's not a he or a she or an it. He's a God.

P: So then we have to use what we have. And the most appropriate is "he."

S: The God . . .

P: Use "he" if you want a pronoun.

S: The one and only God you can only call "God."

P: For sure you can't use "it."

S: You can only call God "God." You can't call him "he," "she," "it" . . .

P: Well, you have to use pronouns, and when you use pronouns . . .

S: Yes, but "God" is a pronoun.

P: It's a proper name.

S: "God" isn't a name.

P: The word "God" is.

S: "God" is a name?

P: Sure. The word "God" is a name for God.

S: "God" isn't a name but a noun.

P: Okay. The word "God" is a noun *used* as a name.

S: Of course. But "God" is God. "God" is not—how can I explain this—*exactly* a pronoun. "God" is a name, but "God" is also just God.

P: You know what you just did a little bit ago? You used a pronoun. You see, the thing is . . .

S: Yes, I used both.

P: That's right. There is no way to talk about anything without using pronouns, so you have to use them with God too.

S: God is both, that's the problem. It's not a problem . . . It's hard to explain.

P: You know why it's so hard to explain?

S: Why?

P: Because it's so simple.

S: Everything is simple at heart.

P: That's right.

S: If you say something is simple, you have to say something else. If you think one plus one is simple, you have to know what numbers are to think that this is simple.

P: That's true. On the other hand, you know what numbers are only because you start out counting—1, 2, 3, 4, 5 . . .

S: Right . . . you have to know what numbers are before you can know that one plus one equals two.

P: Except that . . . Sol—

S: We already talked about this.

P: In the case of God . . . I'm not so interested in numbers at the moment . . .

S: I kind of am.

P: But not at the moment. We're supposed to . . .

S: Yes, at the moment.

P: We're supposed to be talking theology.

S: Yes. But theology is numbers; numbers is theology.

P: Oh come off it!

S: The book of Numbers? (laughter)

P: That's another thing, and you know it.

S: (laughter) I was kidding.

P: What's the number for God?

S: Billions and trillions, nothing. God isn't a number.

P: He is not a number, but he has got a number. How many of you are there?

S: One. There is only one God.

P: Yes. On the other hand, this one God isn't just one blob or point.

S: Like a germ is.

P: He is Father, and Son Jesus, and Holy Spirit.

S: Jesus is part of him.

P: No, not part.

S: Jesus is not God if God is not Jesus.

P: That's what the church teaches.

S: They are together. It's just that Jesus is his own character. It's not like God . . . He is part of God and God is part of him. He has his own brain. He is the Son of God—he has his own brain, he has his own heart. He doesn't have God's brain. He doesn't have anything God has except . . .

P: Well . . .

S: Wait. He does have everything God has. He is different from God. He is not God, and God is part of him. It's just that . . . It's very aggravating.

P: No, it's very simple. Just listen for a moment. There is Jesus, and you say he is a person.

S: He's his own self.

P: Right. And then you have the one he called his Father, and then you've got their Spirit, the Holy Spirit. Then the word God simply applies equally to each of the three or to what they are together.

S: Yes. But Jesus still has his own body. He is not God's body.

P: Jesus is a body. Right. So in that sense, God does have a body.

S: Of course he has a body. He has that body. But Jesus has his own thoughts, and God has his own thoughts. They don't think alike—they do think alike. But Jesus could be watching over one continent, and God could be watching over . . .

P: No, no, no!

S: It's true.

P: No. It isn't true.

S: It could be.

P: It could be, but it isn't. What you have to get over doing is thinking of God as a big blob or this bearded old man.

S: That's not how I imagine it. I just don't imagine Jesus as God. Two separate characters but part of the same . . . But still the same thing.

P: Let's put it this way. Jesus *and* God the Father—you always have to put it that way. If there is a son, there is a father. Right?

S: Well, of course. Most of the time . . .

P: The father may be dead, but there once was a father. Jesus is the Son, and there is God the Father, and there is *God* only in the relationship between them. Can you think that? See, there is you and there is me, and we have a relationship between us . . .

S: Right. But, see, with Jesus and God, they have an equal relationship.

P: That's right. And that relationship is what we call God, with just the word itself.

S: Relationship?

P: Yup.

S: God is a relationship?

P: Between Jesus and his Father.

S: Relationship? Okay. So God the Father . . .

P: And God's Son and God's Spirit, and between them, they are one God.

S: Wait. I knew that. But that's hard to . . .

P: Again, it's hard to hang on to because it's so simple.

S: Right . . . Of course . . . That's the thing—easy things you can lose quite easily; for instance, four plus seven. If you are totally engaged in doing long division, you might forget that. You just have to always have everything in your mind. Well, you can't have everything. You have to store everything in your mind and not get too involved in one thing and not in the other.

P: And God is like that.

Man Ist Was Man Isst

Poppi: Do you smell the turkey cooking?

Solveig: I plan to eat a lot of it.

P: Be careful you don't actually turn into a turkey. There's an old pun that works only in German, where the word for "is" and the word for "eats" sound the same: "*Man ist was man isst*."

S: We're getting off the subject of theology.

P: Not really. Because there *is* a sense in which a person is what she exposes herself to. Whether it is food or words or video games or music or books, you get to be like it, which is why people should go to church.

S: You are not it; you are like it. For instance, if you read a book in the American Girl Series—take Kit, for instance, the doll that I have—in her book, she loves Robin Hood. No, actually, let's change that—she loves Amelia Earhart and wants to be like her. So she does as many things about her as she can, but she can't *be* Amelia Earhart.

P: That's true. But she can get to be very much like Amelia Earhart, and that's why people should go to church, so that they expose themselves to God.

S: Like and like . . . "I like you," which means you're like that person. You never think of them as the same, but they are, in a way. If you say, "I like them," you have to be like them in a way, if you know what I mean.

P: Don't you think you can like someone who is very unlike you?

S: Yes. But you still have something in common.

P: We have to have something in common with whom? Who would be the most important to have something in common with?

S: God.

P: Just God in general, or . . .

S: God not in general but God in person.

P: And which person would that be?

S: Jesus.

P: See, that's how that works.

S: Yes. But it is impossible for anyone to be like Jesus.

P: No, it is not.

S: Oh yes. He is the only person in the world who can do something that is perfect.

P: That's true, but you can do something imperfect that's imperfectly like him. Right?

S: Right. You have to have something in common, so you have to be like him.

P: And if you really like someone, you do get to be more and more like them.

S: So since, for instance, my friends—the more I get to know them or get to like them, the more I get to find things that are in common between us. If you know what I mean. Because if you don't like someone, you're not going to know as much about them as you would if you actually knew them.

Economics

Solveig: Let's continue. Why would Judas have betrayed Jesus?

Poppi: There are two answers to that. Number one, because people do wicked things, and that was the wicked thing that *Judas* did.

S: Yes. But why . . . It seems like it would all fit in one big puzzle. Jesus was so perfect . . . Everyone needs to have something bad happen to them—in a way.

P: Well, now, perfect people can be very irritating.

S: Yeah. It's kind of irritating to know that someone is more perfect than you.

P: Lots of people found Jesus absolutely intolerable. The religious leadership of Israel found him just intolerable because . . .

S: Because he believed he was the Son of God.

P: Yes. And also because if people believed and followed his preaching, it would turn things over. Jesus said, for example, that the widow who gave her little "mite," her little tiny halfpenny, was better than the rich people who gave lots.

S: Of course. Because if a poor person gives away the one—this only small thing that they have, they are being more kind than the wealthy.

P: But how do you suppose the wealthy people felt about that?

S: Not very good; they were probably real mad. Now, here's the thing. In the story "Pennies from Heaven"—I think it's Brothers Grimm—there's this girl. She has one piece of bread, one bonnet, and a little dress, and she goes out—her parents have died. She sees an old man who is starving; she gives him her one piece of bread. She keeps going, and there's a child and he needs a bonnet, and she gives it to him. And then there's another child who needs clothes, and she gives up her clothes and is left with nothing but her underdress. Then pennies fall from heaven because she gave away everything she had.

P: Now, you see, that's socially upsetting.

S: What do you mean?

P: Suppose people took that attitude toward life seriously. Things would fall apart.

S: People would be giving away their things, and then there would be a whole other Depression all over again.

P: The capitalist system, as we call it, is based on greed.

S: If you're not greedy, the whole system would fall apart.

P: Exactly. So you see how Jesus's teaching threatened the whole social and political system.

S: Yes. But then again, it helped. How can something be good and then bad at the same time?

P: It's good . . .

S: Good for some people and bad for others. But it's not a good thing to suffer from something that makes other people good. But it's also a good thing if people who really deserve it get what they need.

P: True. But how about the people who don't deserve it? Should they get what they need?

S: That's what Jesus said.

P: Yes.

S: He loves everyone. He may think that some people deserve more than others, but he wants everyone to be treated equally. But if everyone had the same as everyone, there would be communism all over again. So that wouldn't work either.

P: But you see how communism got started? Jesus preached the kingdom of God, where everyone would be treated equally. What communism was, was an attempt to force God's hand to make the kingdom of God come right away, when we want it.

S: That's a more difficult thing. We were doing fine up until the time communism started.

P: Communists were, of course, atheists. When I said "force God's hand," I didn't mean that literally. They were going to do what Jesus waited for God to do.

S: To make everything equal. But that doesn't mean they can't do that. What Jesus meant was for people to be well off, for everyone to be treated equal.

P: Did he really mean for everyone to be well off? He wasn't.

S: True. But he must have wanted people to be treated equally. If one person was treated badly and everyone else was going on boats around Greece, like you just did . . .

P: I beg your pardon!

S: If one person was being treated so terribly and living on the streets, and everyone else was in the Carribean, Greece and Italy and Venice and Rome and France and England, that person would be helped but not everyone else—but everybody else doesn't deserve it. But that person would be helped by Jesus to make it all equal, so in a way, he wouldn't have to help the other people.

P: That's the problem. Jesus was always on the side of the underdog, and that's another thing that got him crucified. He said—maybe his most famous saying—"The last shall be first and the first shall be last."

S: Yes, of course.

P: In the kingdom of God, those who are ahead now will be behind, and those who are behind now will be ahead. People didn't particularly want to hear that. I don't particularly like to hear it, because I'm more on the ahead side than on the behind side. Right?

S: Right, of course. I go to a good school, and that might mean that I might not go to a good school in heaven.

P: That's the problem.

S: Yes. But you don't want to be treated poorly all the time you are living, because what if there isn't the school in heaven? Then it would be stupid for you to go to a bad school just so you could have a good school in heaven. Of course, your teacher would always be God, and that would help.

P: It would help. (laughter) The Bible as a whole, and not just Jesus, has what some people have called "an option for the poor" and is very suspicious about wealth. It doesn't say that it is positively wicked to be wealthy, but is very suspicious about it. And I have to say—you referred to this lovely cruise that Blanche and I took—there were moments when I worried about this.

S: Are you serious?

P: Yeah. There were moments when I worried about . . .

S: Being in the high life now. But you do want to have a high life in the only time you are actually living.

P: That may be true, but maybe it ought not to be true.

S: You want to have as good a time as possible without getting too selfish and greedy.

P: *If* this life is the only thing there is.

S: Yeah. Perhaps—do you think that he meant that the poor in *heart* will go first to heaven?

P: No.

S: And people who didn't have people to love them, they would be first in heaven. But it didn't matter that you had a high life on earth—that has nothing to do with the first being last and the last being first. The people who nobody really cared for on earth might be the people who God cared for much more. I want to think of it that way so I'll have a good time in heaven. (laughter)

P: I'm sure that Jesus had the poor in heart in mind, but he meant the poor whether physically or in heart. God's on their side, he says.

Prayer, Works, and Hamsters

Solveig: So what do you want to talk about?

Poppi: We had agreed that we would talk about prayer. Praying is talking to God.

S: Right.

P: Does that puzzle you at all?

S: Not particularly.

P: Really?

S: No. I guess if I were someone else . . . As myself, I don't think it is peculiar at all, because I go to church every Sunday and do all of these things, but I guess the people who don't go to church or don't do things about God don't pray.

P: That seems clear.

S: So they might think it was odd—except that it seems like everyone has some sort of religion and has to pray. And it seems—well, Christians pray to God and Jesus, Jews pray to God, the Muslims pray to their God, and everyone else prays too.

P: Not everyone.

S: Not everyone. But lots of people. People pray to Buddha.

P: Well, now—Buddha is an interesting thing. Do you mean the so-called great-vehicle Buddhism?

S: Yeah.

P: They have gods all over the place.

S: Exactly. Even if people have lots of gods, they start praying.

P: But so-called small-vehicle Buddhists don't have gods, so they don't pray.

S: Right. But most of the people do pray.

P: Most people do. Yes.

S: So it doesn't really seem strange to them. What I find strange is—for instance, in the Middle Ages—because I just finished reading *Robin Hood* about a week and a half ago . . . Well, in *Robin Hood*, it's like practically everyone in the whole story is Christian, and of course, they pray all the time. They give oaths to the Virgin Mary; for instance, Robin Hood and his knights say, "We would be scorned by the Virgin herself if we do this kind of thing," and things like that. But then there are the bad people, such as Prince John and the sheriff of Nottingham, and they are Christians—they go to church every Sunday, they have chapels and things—and they are still evil.

P: And how is that possible?

S: They aren't really—well, I guess they are Christians. But they just don't act like it.

P: No. Well, there are two things one wants to say. First, that the difference between bad people and good people is usually relative. You're not entirely a good person either. Nor am I.

S: But I'm not evil.

P: That's true; you're not evil, but you're not purely good either. Right? And neither am I. Or do you think I'm purely good?

S: No.

P: I didn't think so.

S: You steal chocolates. (laughter)

P: I do all sorts of things.

S: You steal chocolates from us and hide them up here.

P: That's true too. And that's for your own good.

S: Why?

P: So that you don't eat the chocolates and get fat and your teeth fall out.

S: Well, whatever. Okay.

P: So one doesn't want to divide the world up into good people and bad people, because the good people do bad things also and the bad people do good things sometimes. Okay?

S: Yes.

P: Do you think there are people who are just sort of evil?

S: I think it has to take something to make you evil, such as maybe jealousy. For instance, with Prince John—going back to *Robin Hood*—King Richard the Lionhearted is off on a crusade; Prince John wants to be king, and that's what turns him evil—in a way.

P: Greed.

S: Greed, yes.

P: Envy.

S: Yes. He wants all the things his brother has. And then he hopes that his brother is killed. He even goes against—because there is a ransom, and Robin Hood and his merry men are collecting the money for the ransom, and Prince John is going against it.

P: You say that there are specific things that make people evil, like envy or greed?

S: Right. For example, in the Bible, when Jesus is crucified, there is something that made Judas betray Jesus.

P: What do you think it was?

S: It could have been jealousy . . . It could have been greed . . . Because he was probably very jealous; he wanted to run things, probably, and he knew that everyone was worshiping Jesus and not him.

P: Not everyone, but the other disciples.

S: Right. Everyone he knew.

P: Or went around with. People used to talk about kinds of sin—mortal sins, the ones that really make you evil, and sort of ordinary sins.

S: Ordinary sins like taking chocolate from the kitchen and taking it up to your study. (laughter)

P: Yes. And two of the mortal sins were jealousy or envy, whichever you want to call it.

S: This is also a common thing. Many people are greedy, and many people are jealous. You could be jealous of someone for getting the . . . For example, last year I know that many people were jealous of a girl in our class for getting the part to be the Statue of Liberty. I wasn't jealous because I didn't really care, but lots of people were.

P: Have you ever been jealous of someone?

S: Oh, sure, sure, plenty of times.

P: You want to watch out for that.

S: Right.

P: Because that's the kind of sin that can make you evil.

S: Well, you've been jealous too. I'm sure, actually, everyone is greedy.

P: I've been greedy, but not often jealous in the sense of being envious.

S: I've never been actually envious, but I have been, like, "Oh, she's so lucky. She has that thing."

P: How does this all relate to the question of prayer?

S: I have no clue. Sometimes when I'm in a discussion, one minute we're talking about politics, and then it turns to wines, for example, for no particular reason at all. And I always wonder how we got to that subject.

P: You were the one who moved us to talk about people, all of whom pray and some of whom are nevertheless evil. Do you find that puzzling?

S: Not particularly. Because some people might think, "Oh, we know it's a good thing to pray," but they don't actually mean what they are doing.

P: You don't think King John actually meant what he was doing?

S: He might have, but he didn't really seem like it, if you know what I mean.

P: Do you mean what you're doing when you pray?

S: Yes.

P: Even when you sort of fire off the table prayer, like you do sometimes?

S: Yes, I mean that. But sometimes I don't want to do it at that particular moment because I'm in the middle of doing something else that I want to finish doing. But when I say it, I mean it.

P: Good.

S: I say what I mean. I mean, I mean what I say. Or whatever.

P: Now let's take the "Come, Lord Jesus" prayer.

S: "Come, Lord Jesus, be our guest . . ."

P: What are you saying when you say that?

S: You are saying, "Come, Lord Jesus, to our table and bless the food."

P: Right.

S: "Come, Lord Jesus, be our guest. And let these gifts to us be blessed."

P: Do you know where that prayer started? It's originally a prayer for the Lord's Supper, and it was in Aramaic, which was the language Jesus spoke. It went *Maranatha*, which is "Come, Lord"—to the Lord's Supper.

S: Cool.

P: And then people extended that to the meals they had in their homes.

S: Well, then, what about that prayer for health and food: (singing) "For health and food and every good, we give thee thanks, O Lord."

P: I don't know where that came from. But it's a nice prayer.

S: So we say, "Everything good that we get—it's all your doing."

P: Do you believe that?

S: Well, everything that we eat, God did make. Is it true that God is the one who bought and paid for the food and brought it to us? No. But it's true that he created the food and the goods too.

P: When your parents or Mimi or I go and buy the food to feed you and ourselves, could we do even that without God?

S: No.

P: I think you're right. So it isn't just that God made the food in the first place. He also . . .

S: Made us.

P: Right.

S: But it's not him who says, "I want to have duck for dinner tonight." Because we have control of ourselves.

P: How much control of ourselves do we have, do you think?

S: I think it's all our doing. We are taught to do something else, if you know what I mean. For instance, at the dinner table, I never sit down, but I could be taught to sit down.

P: I don't know whether that's possible or not.

S: Well, I could be.

P: You'd better start right away then . . .

S: (laughter)

P: Because you're a pain in the neck.

S: Okay. Back to the subject of praying.

P: What about praying would you like to talk about?

S: Let's talk about about the Lord's Prayer. We haven't talked about that.

P: Okay.

S: "Our Father . . ." So we're talking to God . . .

P: And calling him what?

S: Father.

P: Where did we get that word for him?

S: I have no clue.

P: You don't? Jesus himself taught it to his disciples. Jesus's disciples came to him one day and said, "The other rabbis teach their disciples a particular way to pray. You've never taught us a particular way to pray." He said, "When you pray, do it this way."

S: "Our Father . . ."

P: And then he taught them this prayer.

S: Wait. Yes, okay. "Our Father . . ." So he is talking to God.

P: And calling him something.

S: Father. I don't know if Father is exactly the right word. We don't know if God is a man or a female or whatever. Perhaps he is neither.

P: You think he is neither? You know that word. Father . . .

S: He could be like a snail.

P: No, he couldn't. (laughter)

S: I mean like a snail is neither a girl or a boy.

P: There is something special about that word. The Jews thought of God as Father, meaning that he takes care of his people. He is the Father of the Jews; he takes care of his people. But they never, when praying, called him that. They thought that would be too familiar, too fresh.

S: You're supposed to be familiar.

P: We think so, but that it is because of Jesus.

S: Wait. Could we go back to the subject of the prayer, though?

P: We are on the subject of the prayer. I'm going to make an important point here about that first word. It's the special part of the prayer that Jesus taught his disciples. He said, "God is my Father and I'm his Son, and I'm going to let you piggyback on my prayer. I call God Father, and now you can call God Father too, with me."

S: Because he is the Father of everyone and everything too. He's the Father of Puck—a cute little hamster.

P: But however cute Puck is, he doesn't pray.

S: Oh, I wouldn't be so sure about that. I think he prays all the time.

P: How does he do it?

S: He prays that he'll get some cheese, some lettuce. (laughter)

P: I don't hear anything.

S: Oh, he goes "eek."

P: That's not a prayer.

S: How do you know?

P: A prayer is actual talking to God, not just squeaking.

S: Yes, but you don't know . . .

P: I squeak to God all the time too, but that's not praying. Anytime something hurts or . . . But that's not praying.

S: It could be, because you don't know what hamsters talk like.

P: I think we do. They don't talk at all.

S: Oh, but they have their own communication.

P: That may well be.

S: They squeak and that's their communication.

P: Do you think God squeaks back?

S: Maybe. Maybe whoever is praying to God turns into that image.

P: I think that's a bad idea, though people have had it. There was a Greek philosopher long ago named Empedocles who said the Ethiopians think God is black, and we Greeks think he's white, and if donkeys could think, they would think he was a donkey.

S: Well what if he is?

P: There's a sense in which God is, the old theologians used to say, Being. He is the truth and the power behind and above everything—hamsters, galaxies, you, and me. But there's a much more important sense in which we know what God is like because of Jesus, who was a human. God didn't come as a hamster; he came as one of us.

S: If we think of God as a hamster, he would be very cute to stroke.

P: Want to get back to the prayer?

S: Yes.

The Lord's Prayer

Poppi: Okay. "Our Father . . ."

Solvcig: "Our Father, who art in heaven, hallowed be thy name."

P: What does that mean?

S: Does it mean, "Thy name is worshiped?"

P: It means, "Holy be thy name."

S: "Thy kingdom come . . ."

P: Now, what does that mean?

S: Does it mean—sort of like—your kingdom in heaven . . .

P: That's part of it, but there's a more important other part. It goes way back into the Old Testament. God promised that his kingdom would come not just in heaven but that the whole universe would get to be exactly as God wanted it to be.

S: Okay. So, "Thy kingdom come, thy will be done." You want your will to be done . . .

P: Those three petitions more or less mean the same thing.

S: So that what happpens on earth should be like it is in heaven.

P: And when that happens, that will be the kingdom of God.

S: Sure.

P: And then God's name will be hallowed.

S: "Give us this day our daily bread."

P: That's a different kind of petition.

S: Yes. Our daily bread would be Jesus's body.

P: You think it's the Lord's Supper?

S: It could be.

P: It could be. Yes. It probably isn't, but there are lots of scholars who have thought that it might be. Do you know why? Because the word that we translate "daily" in Greek is *epiousion*, and nobody actually knows what that word means. "Daily bread" is just a guess, and another guess is "special bread." We don't know which of those two it is—our regular daily bread—breakfast, dinner, and supper—or the special bread of the Lord's Supper.

S: I think it's the Lord's Supper because . . . Except do you think Jesus could know? When did he teach this prayer? Did he teach it at the Lord's Supper?

P: No.

S: How would he have known that he was to be crucified?

P: Well, he was a prophet, and that's one thing that prophets do.

S: All right. It could be that. "Forgive us our trespasses as we forgive those who trespass against us . . ." That's actually not true—well, you don't always forgive people.

P: Do you think you'll get forgiven if you don't forgive?

S: Maybe.

P: That's risking it.

S: See, if they don't know that you don't forgive them . . .

P: The point is not that if I don't forgive you, you won't forgive me. The point is that if I don't forgive you, *God* won't forgive me. See, the prayer is to God—"Forgive us our sins as we forgive *other* people."

S: I forgive lots of things, but I don't forgive every single thing.

P: Well, you should. It's very dangerous, not just with God but with ourselves. Sins against us that we don't forgive sit in our souls and just sort of rot there.

S: I forgive most things. It's only one or two things.

P: What are the one or two things you don't?

S: I can't say it, but you know what I mean.

P: You have to forgive that too. I have a very hard time doing it, but I have to try.

S: Yes. You have to try.

P: So do you.

Further to the Lord's Prayer

Solveig: "And lead us not into temptation."

Poppi: Does that one cause you any problem?

S: Yes. Oh sure, I'm tempted plenty of times. For instance, when Mimi told me to get down from the porch railing, I stepped right back up on it.

P: What kind of sin is that? You were not just tempted; you fell.

S: I didn't fall.

P: I didn't mean you fell off the railing. I mean you weren't just tempted, but you actually did it. Right?

S: Right. (laughter) Puck is tempted quite a lot, and he fell too. He's tempted quite often to just climb out when I open his cage door. He's always tempted to climb up on the cage door, and once, he was tempted to go down the stairs in his exercise ball.

P: But the thing about that petition, Solveig, is that it asks *God* not to tempt us.

S: He wants to see if we really can be trusted, I think. You say you wouldn't trust me around the corner, but how would God feel about that?

P: Can you think of a story in the Bible in which God tempted someone?

S: I can think of the devil.

P: But can you think of a story in the Bible in which God tested someone? You said that God wanted to test us, right?

S: Adam and Eve.

P: That's a good one.

S: But we've talked about that already.

P: He put that tree there and said you can't eat from that tree. He didn't give them any explanation of why they couldn't. It was a pure test of whether they would obey or not.

S: And . . .

P: They didn't.

S: I guess Noah's ark is kind of—well, it wasn't a test, but it was . . .

P: You know the one famous story of God's testing is the story we heard part of read yesterday morning at the service.

S: Abraham.

P: Abraham and Isaac. Right. Supposing that Abraham had actually killed Isaac. That would have been a terrible thing. So in a sense, God told Abraham to do a terrible thing just to see if he would obey. God never intended Abraham actually to do it.

S: Because he said if you don't do it, you'll be blessed.

P: Well, that's the problem in the story, isn't it?

S: You'll be blessed, but not to do it, so . . . But he didn't do it.

P: But he showed that he would have done it if God really wanted it.

S: But he knew God hadn't really . . .

P: Well, I don't suppose that Abraham actually knew that. That story is so puzzling and such a terrible story that it actually has its own name. There are just a few stories in the Bible that have their own names—the exodus of the people from Egypt, the crucifixion . . .

S: The resurrection.

P: The resurrection, and the *Akedah*. That's Hebrew for "Binding," and it's the name that Jews and Christians have for this particular story.

S: All right. So back to the subject of prayer. "But deliver us from evil." That would be, "Take us away from doing evil."

P: It could. More likely, however, it means . . .

S: It has to do with temptation, though. "Don't let us be tempted."

P: That's a good thought, but you know, there's something funny about that one too.

S: What?

P: A more accurate translation would probably be, "Deliver us from the evil one"—the devil.

S: So we don't actually know what was on Jesus's mind when he said that?

P: We don't know what was on Jesus's mind. But we can do our best to translate the words he used. See, the Lord's Prayer has been translated twice. Jesus spoke Aramaic, and the New Testament is written in Greek, so in the New Testament, the prayer has been translated from Aramaic to Greek. And then, of course, we pray it in English.

S: Yes, but in other languages too. Because at the cathedral, for example, they have Language Day, and you can pray in whatever language you know. And I wanted to translate the Lord's Prayer into Pig Latin . . .

P: You wanted to translate it into Pig Latin? Do people actually pray the Lord's Prayer in Pig Latin?

S: Maybe.

P: You ought to learn the Lord's Prayer in Greek.

S: I don't really want to do it in Greek. (attempts it in Pig Latin)

P: Do you think it might be blasphemous to make words for the Lord's Prayer in Pig Latin? If you want to do it in real Latin, that's another matter.

S: Pig Latin is a beginning.

P: There's one other point I want to tell you about the Lord's Prayer, and then we can drop this, if you have some other thing you want to talk about.

S: Yes, I do.

P: "Lead us not into temptation." That's another place where there might be a different translation. And in fact, in the modern English translations there is, "Save us from the time of trial."

S: Save us from the time of trial? When we're being tested to see if we go to heaven or hell?

P: That would be a time of trial.

S: Yes, it definitely would.

P: Now, do you think it's how we come out of the test that decides whether we are saved or not?

S: No.

P: Not really.

S: Do you think of where you might go after you die as two places or three places? I think of it as three places.

P: What three is that?

S: Heaven, purgatory, and hell.

P: So you hold to the doctrine of purgatory?

S: Yes.

P: You know that is very controversial.

S: Why? It's in Dante, isn't it?

P: Well, it's in Dante, yes. But of course, Dante isn't exactly in the Bible.

S: No. But he's still . . .

P: The thing about purgatory is that it's a very reasonable idea. It's just that we don't know if it is true.

S: Except . . . Maybe God thinks that you should just go to two places. If you are bad, he has no patience with you at all, and he will just sort you to go to heaven or hell. I think that is reasonable enough.

P: That God is impatient?

S: Yes.

P: That's where I think the notion of purgatory is reasonable. I don't think the Bible talks about God's being impatient in quite that way.

S: If he isn't impatient, maybe he doesn't want us to spend time thinking about where we should go.

P: You know that plate that your mother and father gave us that hangs on the wall in the dining room?

S: Yes.

P: Remember what it says on it?

S: I don't remember what it says.

P: It says, "I desire not the death of the wicked."

S: "As I live, saith the Lord God, I have no pleasure in the death of the wicked."

P: Right. So the biblical God takes no pleasure in sending people to hell, and that's why I think that purgatory is a reasonable idea. The problem is we don't have any way of knowing whether the purgatory idea is true or not.

S: It's just Dante's idea.

P: Well, it was older than Dante.

S: It was?

P: Yes.

S: All right, then! We haven't finished the prayer yet. But Dante thought of some very good thoughts.

P: What other good thoughts did Dante have?

S: He had plenty of good thoughts. He thought of hell in a certain way . . .

P: Have you read Dante?

S: No.

P: How do you know about it?

S: Well, Daddy has talked about it at the dinner table. We read that booklet about fifty times. Maybe not fifty; maybe once or twice.

P: Your dad likes Dante, doesn't he?

S: Yes. Well, see, I think of Dante as a theologian, in a way.

P: He was a very great theologian.

S: Yeah, I know. I'm saying that he kind of liked to make up things he wasn't quite sure about, if you know what I mean.

He thought of hell in a certain way that hadn't been thought of before—what we were just talking about. Well, let's get back to the subject of prayer.

P: Okay. Are there other prayers besides the Lord's Prayer that are big important ones?

S: The creed. What's it called? We do it on Sunday.

P: The Nicene Creed.

S: The Nicene Creed.

The Nicene Creed

Poppi: That's a kind of prayer, but it's a different kind of prayer, isn't it?

Solveig: Yeah.

P: The Lord's Prayer is made up of what? Of petitions. We're always asking for something.

S: Right.

P: In the creed, we don't ask anything at all.

S: We're telling what we know.

P: Right. About him.

S: About three things.

P: About God, in any case.

S: Right. Jesus and the Holy Spirit, which we have talked about, so we don't need to bring up the subject of the Holy Spirit again.

P: Okay. The point I wanted to make was that there are prayers that don't involve asking God for stuff.

S: Sure.

P: The creed is one like that.

S: We're asking God for things for other people.

P: That's true. But the creed doesn't even do that, does it?

S: No.

P: But it's still a prayer.

S: All right. So you say it, and I'll explain what it means. Because I don't know the whole thing. I have most of it memorized, but not the whole thing. Well, I'll join in. I just can't remember the first line.

P and S: "We believe in God, the Father Almighty, maker of all things, seen and unseen."

P: I get mixed up. Do you know why?

S: Why?

P: Because as a child, I learned the creed in a different translation.

S: What did you learn?

P: It's like the Lord's Prayer. The one we automatically use is "Our Father, who art in heaven, hallowed be thy name." That's an old kind of English.

S: Right.

P: There's a modern translation that doesn't use that kind of English—"hallowed be your name, your kingdom come . . ."

S: "Your will be done on earth as it is in heaven."

135

S and P: "Give us this day our daily bread, and forgive us our sins as we forgive those who sin against us. And save us from the time of trial . . ."

S: I like the older one much better.

P: Everyone likes the older one much better. But anyway, what I was saying was that it's the same way with the creed. With the creed, the one you learned is the new one, and the one I learned is the old one, which is why I get it mixed up.

S: What's the old one? Oh, I want to do the one I know because . . .

P: Okay. You go ahead then.

S: Well, I don't have it memorized. Do you have it in the Bible somewhere? I have most of it memorized.

P: It's not in the Bible.

S: I mean in the prayer book. The Book of Common Prayer has it, doesn't it?

P: Yes. We have it—there.

S: Okay. Back to this . . . "We believe in one God, the Father, the Almighty . . ."

P: Why do you suppose the creed insists upon there being one God?

S: Because there is only one God.

P: Most people think there are many. Right?

S: Right. "We believe in one God, the Father, the Almighty . . ."

P: Any problem about that?

S: What's the problem?

P: I'm asking you.

S: Is there a problem?

P: Well, there's a funny question . . .

S: What's the question?

P: We talked about that before . . . Could God make two and two be five?

S: Right. No.

P: So almighty doesn't necessarily mean . . .

S: But it could be that two plus two is five because God wanted it to be that.

P: I don't think so.

S: If he had made it that way in the very, very beginning, it could be that now he couldn't suddenly go and change it.

P: Aha! Okay

S: Because that would change all the numbers of the whole—numerous numbers would be wrong. So . . . "Maker of heaven and earth." There's a difference between them, obviously.

P: What is it?

S: Heaven is more paradise; earth is a test.

P: A test? Okay.

S: "Of all that is, seen and unseen."

P: Is there a lot of stuff that is unseen?

S: Plenty.

P: Like what?

S: Him.

P: He didn't make himself.

S: Yes, he did. (laughter)

P: No. God didn't *make* himself.

S: He's just there.

P: He's just there. But are there creatures, things that God made, that are unseen?

S: Sure. We can't see—at the moment, I'm not looking at a big cheetah sitting right in front of me.

P: But if there were one here, he would be seen.

S: Right. You can't see the devil.

P: I suppose not.

S: Unless you're dead.

P: How about angels?

S: Not in this very room, you can't. But downstairs you can; there are plenty on that tree.

P: But those aren't real.

S: Yes, but you're still seeing angels. If you watch *A Wonderful Life*, you're sure to see angels.

P: But are proper angels visible?

S: No.

P: They can get to be visible.

S: Earth is like a place where he wants you to wonder about things, to learn things. I've seen a picture of angels with big ears. I never knew they have big ears like elephants.

P: I don't think they do have big ears like elephants.

S: How do you know if you've never seen one?

138

P: We only know about angels because of the Bible. In the Bible, when they do become visible, they look like shining people.

S: Okay. "Of all that is seen and unseen. We believe in one Lord, Jesus Christ." So "one" again.

P: Yes.

S: "The only Son of God . . ."

P: He doesn't have a whole bunch.

S: "Eternally begotten of the Father . . ."

P: Eternally begotten? Now, Solveig, when your father begat you, that happened at a particular time.

S: November 3rd, two o'clock in the morning.

P: That's when you were born.

S: (laughter)

P: And they begat you nine months before that. Right?

S: Right.

P: But Jesus is *eternally* begotten of the Father. That is to say, there never was a time when he wasn't with the Father. His being begotten of the Father doesn't have a date like your being begotten of your parents has a date.

S: Okay. Back to the creed. "We believe in one Lord, Jesus Christ, the only Son of God, the only begotten of the Father."

P: "Eternally begotten."

S: Now, "the only Son of God." There's a problem with that. We're all sons of God.

P: Not by nature.

S: I'm a *daughter* of God, but we're all . . .

P: But you're an adopted child of God.

S: I am?

P: God had only one child.

S: *Real* child—except he didn't have a seed? Did he?

P: I don't know what you mean.

S: A seed that went through his body.

P: No. We are God's children because we're with Jesus. Jesus is God's only begotten Son, and we are Jesus's brothers and sisters. That's how we are God's children, by way of Jesus.

S: "God from God, light from light, true God from true God . . ."

P: Those almost all say the same thing over again, don't they?

S: Yes.

P: By way of nailing it down.

S: "Begotten not made . . ."

P: God didn't *make* Jesus; he *begat* him. He made *you* and begat the Son.

S: "Of one being with the Father . . ."

P: Do you understand that?

S: It's the only one, actually. He sits at the right hand of the Father, so, in a way, he is the only one with God?

P: Well, this word "being."

S: Right. Human being—you're being someone, you're being . . .

P: Someone.

S: Right.

P: So when you ask, What is Jesus being? what's the answer?

S: Jesus is being Jesus.

P: Yes. And he is also being some *kind* of thing. What kind of thing?

S: God.

P: See how it works?

S: I still think the Holy Spirit should be between Jesus and God, but . . .

P: A lot of people do.

S: You remember we talked about that before. But that's not what we're talking about. "One being with the Father. Through him all things were made."

P: Doesn't that bring any problem at all? About all things being made *through* Jesus?

S: Yes.

P: What?

S: Well, I would like to say Jesus is not the one who wrote the many movies Daddy is writing. He did not write your systematic theology.

P: That's certainly true. But that's the same point we had earlier, isn't it? In one way, we do what we do, but we would not do it if it were not for God.

S: Right. But it's not the same for Jesus.

P: And that's why it is in the creed; all things were made *through* him.

S: But I don't think . . .

P: We're made through Jesus; he's not made through us.

S: But there were many more people before Jesus.

P: Were there really? If he's *eternally* begotten of the Father . . .

Time and Eternity

Solveig: But he wasn't just sitting up there on the right hand of the Father for trillions . . . Well, there weren't even *years*, exactly.

Poppi: Right! There weren't even years, exactly.

S: Oh my gosh! I hate to think about the fact that he was just sitting up there forever. There was no beginning . . .

P: But if there is no beginning, then it isn't "forever and ever."

S: That's what I don't understand. It is hard for me to think about the fact that . . . We're just living and then we're gone. It's hard for me to imagine ever and ever. There had to be a beginning somewhere; that's why I just can't imagine that there is ever and ever and ever.

P: But that's not how Christians think about eternity. The way you're talking about it, and the way most people do, it's as if there is a long line on which events succeed each other, kerplunk, kerplunk, kerplunk. And on the line, here's the point where Robert Jenson starts up, and after a while, there's no more Robert Jenson, and so on. This kind of line is called a timeline.

S: Yes.

P: Okay. The thing is that God doesn't have a timeline.

S: No, he doesn't.

P: That's the difference between us.

S: But there has always been an ever and ever.

P: When you say there has always been an ever and ever, you are supposing the timeline.

S: But how do you imagine eternity?

P: You don't imagine it.

S: Okay. Then let's just change the subject, if there is nothing to do about it.

P: There is something to do about it. But you can't *imagine* it.

Back to the Creed

Solveig: Okay. "One being with the Father," who came down "for us and for our salvation." He saved us and came down from heaven under "the power of the Holy Spirit."

Poppi: When did he do that?

S: When he was born by the Virgin Mary.

P: Because that's what comes next.

S: "By the power of the Holy Spirit. He became incarnate from the Virgin Mary . . ."

P: You said earlier that you thought the Holy Spirit should be between the Father and the Son.

S: Yeah.

P: See, in a way he is. Here he pops up.

S: But there has to be an explanation before . . . There should be an explanation before in the center they say . . .

P: You think there should be something said about the Holy Spirit, rather than just popping him in there.

S: Yes.

P: That might have been a good idea.

S: "He became incarnate from the Virgin Mary and was made man. For our sake, he was crucified under Pontius Pilate, he suffered death . . ."

P: Why do you suppose it mentions Pontius Pilate?

S: Because Pontius was the one who killed him.

P: But why does it bother to mention who killed him?

S: Because that person might be scorned forever.

P: Not really. Do you know how the Romans kept dates?

S: How?

P: We have a number series, and we're up to 2003 now.

S: In a few days it will be 2004.

P: They didn't have that.

S: And it's closer than I thought! Oh my gosh, two more days!

P: And then we'll all start forgetting what date it is.

S: Yes, I worried about that this morning. I was just thinking about when we get back to school next Monday—exactly a week from now—and thinking that maybe our teacher might by accident put 2003 on the board.

P: She might very well. Anyway, that's off the point. The Romans didn't have a single number series of years. They gave their dates by reference to who was ruling at the time. So the reason that Pontius Pilate is in the creed is to date Jesus's crucifixion.

S: But then there is a timeline. That's the problem.

P: There is a timeline for us. And as Jesus is human, he's on a timeline.

S: All right, there is a timeline, then.

P: For us.

S: Okay. So then, "He suffered death and was buried. On the third day, he rose from the dead, in accordance with the Scriptures. He ascended into heaven."

P: Anything you want to think about there?

S: No.

P: Okay.

S: "He ascended into heaven . . ."

P: How did he do that?

S: He was the Son of God. He can do anything.

P: Okay. (laughter)

S: "And is seated at the right hand of the Father"—and that doesn't necessarily mean the right hand; it might be the right side. "He will come again in glory to judge the living and the dead, and his kingdom will have no end."

P: There's that kingdom of God again that we pray for in the Lord's Prayer.

S: "We believe in the Holy Spirit." Finally . . . I think it should be between, though.

P: We said that before.

S: What about you? What do you think?

P: Actually, I agree with you too. I think that Father, Spirit, Son is probably a better arrangement.

S: Have you thought that since you were born, or have you . . .

P: No, just the last couple of years.

S: You did?

P: Yeah.

S: When you started reading all these theologians?

P: I am a theologian; I don't just read them. It's an idea that's floating around with a lot of us these days. Colin Gunton—our friend who just died—was very big on having the Holy Spirit in there right from the start.

S: He's probably listening to us right now.

P: Could be.

S: "We believe in the Holy Spirit, the Lord, the giver of life."

P: That tells what the Holy Spirit does. We've talked about this before—spirit is . . .

S: Something that everyone has.

P: The liveliness.

S: You have spirit, but then there is the Holy Spirit.

P: Right, Spirit is liveliness, and the Holy Spirit is the one who gives liveliness.

S: Okay. "Proceeds from the Father and the Son . . ."

P: What does that mean? "Proceeds from the Father and the Son"?

S: He *works* from the Father and the Son? He *does* for the Father and the Son?

P: Well, you see, with the Son in the second article, it is "begotten, not made." That's how the Son has his being. Then here is the way the Spirit has his being—he "proceeds," he moves out from, he blows out from God.

S: He does?

P: He's God's wind. He's the liveliness of God.

S: "With the Father and Son, he is worshiped and glorified. He has spoken through the prophets. We believe in one, holy, catholic, and apostolic church; we acknowledge one baptism for the forgiveness of sin; we look for the resurrection of the dead and the life of the world to come. Amen."

P: Amen. Now, is there anything about that you want to talk about?

S: Well, "we believe in one, holy, catholic, and apostolic church"—that is clear.

P: You think that's all clear?

S: What we just said is clear. "We acknowledge one baptism for the forgiveness of sin."

P: Why shouldn't there be two baptisms?

S: Baptism is about one God, one Jesus, one everything, one being . . .

P: Okay.

S: It's one wholeness. "We look for the resurrection of the dead . . ."

P: When the kingdom comes, the people who have died will not be left out of it.

S: Right. "And the life of the world to come."

P: When we come to that part of the creed in church, what do most people do? You do it. You cross yourself, right?

S: Because the life of the world to come would be Jesus's life—Father, Son, and Holy Spirit. Here's what I like about crossing: the Holy Spirit's in the middle. (crossing herself)

P: You do it that way?

S: How do you do it?

P: I do it that way too. But I've never thought about it being connected to the Trinity in that way, with the Holy Spirit being in the middle. That's cool.

Lent

Solveig: Okay. Ask me . . .

Poppi: No. You were the one who said you had something to talk about. What do you want to talk about?

S: Lent.

P: Lent. Okay. What do you want to say about it?

S: You remember? The long period before Christmas?

P: Advent.

S: Yes. So now I want to know about Lent.

P: What do you want to know about it?

S: Why do people give up things for Lent?

P: There is a long tradition of denying oneself things that one likes in order to concentrate one's attention on more important things.

S: Tell the story of Lent—forty days and forty nights.

P: You remember at the time of the Easter Vigil? Oh wait, you don't go to the Easter Vigil yet.

S: I go to Maundy Thursday and Good Friday, but not that late on Saturday.

P: Okay. That late service is the time that many people are baptized, and in the early church, just about everyone—unless it was an emergency, if someone was dying or something—everyone was baptized at the Easter Vigil.

S: Every year?

P: Yes. Mostly grownups were baptized at the Easter Vigil. So it got to be that the time before Easter was the time they were prepared for baptism. You understand that most people were baptized as adults. Most people came into the church because they were converted; they were pagans to begin with, and then they became Christians. Like your father, who was baptized as an adult, so most people were baptized as

149

adults. That was the normal thing. Infant baptism is a kind of exception.

S: If you are baptized when you are a baby, you have no clue.

P: Right. So most people were being prepared to be baptized just before Easter. The preparation for baptism included fasting, which means giving up things to concentrate on what you are about. Then the next idea was that people noticed the analogy between giving up things for concentration and what Jesus did in the forty days in the wilderness. So they made the period of preparation be forty days—and that's Lent.

S: Okay.

P: Now it is only for a few people that Lent gets to be that period of preparation. So it has come to be that everybody acts as if they were going to be baptized at the Easter Vigil. And in fact, everybody there repeats their baptismal promises and gets sprinkled with baptismal water, so it's sort of a reenactment of baptism. And so Lent is preparation for being baptized or for reenacting your baptism, and that means giving up things. Now, you know your family, and Blanche and I, are not very much at giving up things . . .

S: Especially it's hard for Mimi, because her birthday is coming up.

P: But we ought to be better at that. If you gave up something for Lent, what would it be?

S: Setting the table. (laughter)

P: You give up things you like.

S: What I would give up is perfectly hopeless, because I just did it Saturday.

P: It's a little late for this Lent, so let's think about the next.

S: *Lizzie McGuire*. But I don't watch it during the school week anyway.

P: Is that a TV show?

S: Yeah. I wouldn't watch that during the school week anyway, because I'm not allowed to.

P: I think for TV shows to count, it would have to be more or less all of them.

S: But that's impossible. Because we watch the news.

P: Maybe you could just watch the news.

S: That's impossible for me because that's the only time I watch movies.

P: It has to hurt a little bit or it doesn't count.

S: During school break is the only time . . .

P: That's the kind of rationalization . . .

S: I'm not doing it then.

P: Is there anything else?

S: I can't think of anything. Let's get on with the story.

P: That *is* the story we're now talking about—you.

S: The story of Lent—Jesus.

P: The forty days? In Jesus's case, it went the other way around. First, he was baptized, and then he was forty days

151

in the wilderness. What happened when Jesus was baptized, do you remember?

S: No. I don't remember.

John the Baptist

Poppi: Well, John the Baptist was out there on the Jordan River, and people came out to him to be baptized for repentance and forgiveness of sins. One day, Jesus showed up. This was his first appearance in public. He had been growing up and working as a carpenter. This was the beginning of his ministry. Jesus asked to be baptized, and John said, "You don't need to be baptized. You haven't done anything to repent of." And Jesus said, "Never mind. We'll do it anyway." So they went down into the water, and when Jesus had been dunked by John and stood up, there was a voice that was heard.

Solveig: But how was that possible? Because didn't he already have disciples?

P: No. He only started gathering disciples after his baptism.

S: Okay.

P: We know very little about what Jesus was doing for the first thirty years of his life.

S: How did anyone know he was Jesus, then?

P: That was his name.

S: But how did they know he was God's Son?

P: They didn't.

S: How did John the Baptist know?

P: It doesn't say.

S: Do you have any guesses?

P: Well, John was a prophet, so presumably he knew it the same way prophets in general knew.

S: Okay. So then what happened?

P: So then Jesus was baptized, and there was a voice . . .

S: Yes?

P: In the earliest one of the Gospels to be written . . .

S: Which one was that?

P: Mark. It seemed as if only Jesus heard the voice, as if the voice was speaking just to him. But then in Matthew and Luke, the voice speaks not just to Jesus but to everyone who is standing around. The voice said, "This is my beloved Son," and people saw a dove above Jesus's head, between the voice and Jesus. In paintings of Jesus's baptism, you will see Jesus standing in the water, and up above you'll see a cloud with rays of light coming from it to indicate the voice, and then halfway between the cloud and Jesus there will be the dove. That was the installation of Jesus into his work of preaching and healing.

S: So then everyone knew who he was because of the voice?

P: Not everyone, but those who heard the voice and believed it. It would be perfectly possible to have heard the voice and to have said, "It's just thundering or something."

S: So then . . .

P: So then Jesus, as the story goes on, was driven out into the wilderness by the Holy Spirit. That wasn't necessarily very far, because the part of the Jordan River where John was, was already more or less wilderness on both sides. It just means he went a little ways into the desert.

S: With his followers?

P: No. He didn't have any followers yet.

S: But you said that after his baptism . . .

P: After the forty days.

S: Okay. But that was right before his death.

P: No. There were three years to go. The usual under-standing is that Jesus's ministry was about three years long. It started with his baptism and ended with the crucifixion.

Forty Days and Forty Nights

Solveig: But forty days and forty nights?

Poppi: They were just in the wilderness.

S: Right. After forty days and forty nights comes Easter and Good Friday . . .

P: In the Christian liturgical calendar, but not in the life of Jesus. Like I said, it's the other way around—the forty days comes after his baptism.

S: Okay.

P: Have we got that straightened out?

S: Yes.

P: So then, in the forty days, what happened?

S: He was tempted.

P: What were the three temptations? Do you remember?

S: No.

P: The first one was that the devil . . .

S: I know that, but I don't know what . . .

P: The forty days were without food.

S: Right.

P: So the devil said to him, "If you're the Son of God, whomp up some food for yourself; change some of these stones to bread."

S: He was not a sorcerer.

P: So he didn't do it.

S: Then what did the devil say?

P: Jesus answered the devil, "It is written"—by the way, all of Jesus's answers to the devil start out, "It is written," referring to the Bible—"'Man does not live by bread alone but by every word that comes from the mouth of God.'" That is to say, I can get along without bread, but I can't get along without God and hearing from him. So that temptation didn't work.

S: All right.

P: Then the next one the devil tried—he took him up to the top of a mountain. Where that mountain is, is a little hard to say because there aren't any mountains in the vicinity—but anyway, he took him up on a mountain . . .

S: Well, that mountain could have been blown over by now.

P: Or they could have been instantaneously transported, since this was the devil at work. Anyway, he took him up to the mountain, from which he could see the world's great cities, and he said—and this is sort of scary—"All those cities belong to me."

S: That's not scary.

P: What the devil said is that they are in his control.

S: Okay. And?

P: Jesus didn't contradict him at that point, so the devil said, "Those cities are mine, and if you will worship me, I will give them to you."

S: "If you will worship me, I'll give them to you"?

P: Yes. "You will become king of the world."

S: Okay.

P: Jesus resisted that temptation too. He said, "It is written"—starting off the same way—"'You shall worship the Lord your God and him only shall you serve.'" He quoted the first commandment.

S: Right.

P: The devil had one more shot.

S: And what did he say?

P: He took him to Jerusalem and to the tower of the temple. And from the tower of the temple, he looked down to the pavement, and this time the devil quotes scripture himself. He quotes a passage that says, "He shall give his angels charge concerning you lest you dash your foot against a stone." "So," he said, "if you are the Son of God, jump."

S: What does that mean, though, what he said?

P: The devil's idea in quoting scripture is that if Jesus is really the Son of God, he can just jump off the temple, and God will send angels to catch him before he hurts himself. The idea was that Jesus was to prove that he was the Son of God by doing this. Jesus said, "It is written, 'You shall not tempt the Lord your God.'" That is to say, you shall not test him by saying, "I'm going to jump off, and you prove I'm the Son of God by catching me."

S: Don't put the Lord God to the test?

P: Yes.

S: I was just reading the Ten Commandments the other night, and it said, "Thou shall not put the Lord your God to the test"—or something like that.

P: That's a different one: "You shall not take the name of the Lord your God in vain."

S: Maybe it's part of the fifth commandment.

P: Maybe.

S: All right. Keep going.

P: That was the end. The devil gave up for the meantime.

S: What do you mean by meantime?

P: There are a couple of more times.

S: Yes, obviously.

P: So that was the temptation of those forty days . . .

S: And forty nights.

P: When people took Lent very seriously—as they really used to and still do some places—the idea was that you gave up things during Lent to the point that your life during Lent got to be a little like Jesus's life in the wilderness.

S: Gave up?

P: Well, as much as you could.

S: Of course, you have to . . .

P: You know what Mardi Gras is?

S: Right.

P: It's Fat Tuesday, and that meant that on that Tuesday, the day before Lent starts, you stoked up on food and drink because Lent really was self discipline.

Anything More?

Solveig: Okay. Anything more you want to talk about now?

Poppi: It's you who has to decide that.

S: Well, we've talked about a lot of things.

P: We have indeed.

S: I can't think of anything.

P: Okay. Then we will stop.

158